rib-tick

M+A-I÷H

Strengthening Basic Skills with Jokes, Comics, and Riddles

GRADE 3

Credits

Author: Darcy Andries

Editor: Barrie Hoople

Cover and Layout Design: Chasity Rice

Inside Illustrations: Chris Sabatino

Cover Illustration: Rich Powell

This book has been correlated to state, national, and Canadian provincial standards. Visit *www.carsondellosa.com* to search for and view its correlations to your standards.

ISBN: 978-1-60418-140-1

Table of Contents

Skills Matrix (Based on NCTM Content Strands)

Page Number	Number & Operations	Algebra	Geometry	Measurement	Data Analysis & Probability	Page Number	Number & Operations	Algebra	Geometry	Measurement	Data Analysis & Probability
4	√					39	√				
5	√			√		40	√				
6	√					41	√				
7	√					42	√				
8	√					43	√				
9	√					44	√			√	
10	√					45				√	
11	√					46	√			√	
12	√					47				√	
13	√					48				√	
14	√					49				√	
15	√					50	√			√	
16	√					51				√	
17	√					52			√		
18	√					53			√		
19	√					54			√		
20	√					55			√		
21	√					56			√		
22	√					57			√		
23	√					58			√		
24	√					59			√		
25	√					60	√		√	√	
26	√					61	√		√	√	
27	√					62			√		
28	√					63	√	√			
29	√					64	√	√			
30	√					65	√	√			
31	√					66	√	√			
32	√					67	√	√			
33	√					68	√	√			
34	√					69	√	√			
35	√					70	√				√
36	√					71	√				√
37	√					72	√			√	√
38	√					73	√			√	√

There's No Comparison

Use >, <, or = to compare each pair of numbers. Circle the letter next to the greater number. If the numbers are equal, circle both letters. To solve the riddle, write the circled letters in order on the answer lines.

1. **T** 759 ◯ 258 **S**

2. **H** 161 ◯ 161 **E**

3. **B** 25 ◯ 29 **Y**

4. **B** 230 ◯ 320 **A**

5. **R** 685 ◯ 594 **M**

6. **E** 267 ◯ 267 **S**

7. **M** 141 ◯ 139 **B**

8. **A** 342 ◯ 324 **B**

9. **M** 573 ◯ 753 **R**

10. **L** 206 ◯ 208 **T**

11. **K** 882 ◯ 822 **D**

12. **I** 425 ◯ 254 **S**

13. **A** 330 ◯ 338 **D**

14. **N** 980 ◯ 995 **S**

Why do baby goats know how to compare numbers?

Answer: Because ___ ___ ___   ___ ___ ___ ___

___ ___ ___ ___ ___ "___ ___ ___ ___ ___ ___"

Tools of the Trade

Circle the best estimate for each problem. To solve the riddle, write each circled letter in order on the answer lines.

1. Length of a basketball court
   - L. About 9 feet
   - M. About 90 feet

2. Number of doors in a house
   - U. About 10
   - V. About 100

3. Number of minutes in 1 year
   - L. About 525,000 minutes
   - M. About 50,000 minutes

4. Number of liters in 1 gallon
   - T. About 4
   - U. About 1

5. Weight of a humpback whale
   - H. About 700 tons
   - I. About 70,000 pounds

6. Cost of a candy bar
   - P. About $1.00
   - Q. About $10.00

7. Number of pounds in 1 kilogram
   - K. About 20 pounds
   - L. About 2 pounds

8. Weight of a cat
   - I. About 10 pounds
   - J. About 50 pounds

9. Height of a car
   - E. About 5 feet
   - F. About 15 feet

10. Weight of a textbook
    - Q. About 10 pounds
    - R. About 1 pound

11. Height of Mount Everest
    - S. About 30,000 feet
    - T. About 3,000 feet

What tools do you need in math class?

TOOLBOX

Answer: " ___ ___ ___ ___ ___ – ___ ___ ___ ___ ___ ___ ___ "

Every Dog Has Its Day

Round each number to the nearest ten. Match each answer with the correct letter in the key. To solve the riddle, write the letters in order on the answer lines.

1.	594	_____
2.	455	_____
3.	1,723	_____
4.	2,787	_____
5.	7,865	_____
6.	879	_____
7.	342	_____
8.	3,954	_____
9.	1,698	_____
10.	776	_____

340 = O
460 = H
590 = S
780 = E
880 = O
1,700 = L
1,720 = A
2,790 = M
3,950 = D
7,870 = P

What kind of dog likes to take a bath?

Answer: A " ___ ___ ___ ___ – ___ ___ ___ ___ ___ ___ "

Round each number to the nearest hundred. Match each answer with the correct letter in the key. To solve the riddle, write the letters in order on the answer lines.

11.	886	_____
12.	842	_____
13.	657	_____
14.	3,179	_____
15.	1,920	_____
16.	6,059	_____
17.	4,846	_____

700 = L
800 = U
900 = B
1,900 = D
3,200 = L
4,800 = G
6,100 = O

What kind of dog chases red objects?

Answer: A " ___ ___ ___ – ___ ___ ___ "

Standard Form Puzzle

The numbers below are in expanded form. Solve each problem by writing the numbers in standard form. Then, complete the crossword puzzle.

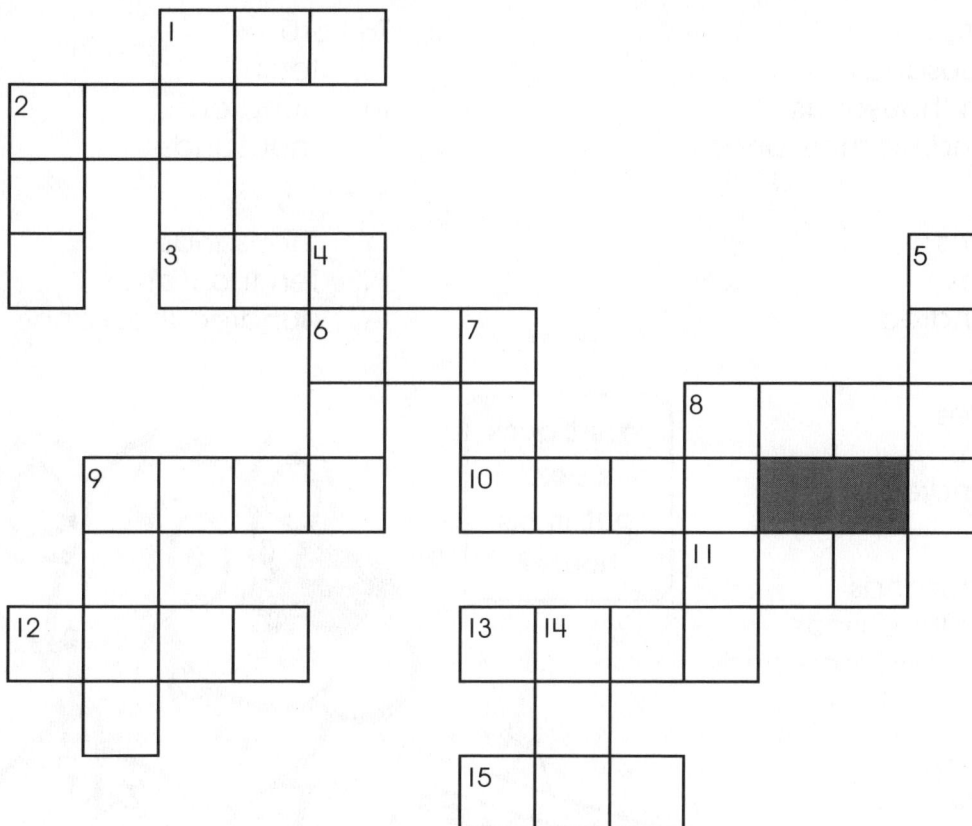

Across

1. $600 + 10 + 8 =$
2. $200 + 70 + 8 =$
3. $400 + 80 + 5 =$
6. $700 + 3 =$
8. $7,000 + 300 + 6 =$
9. $5,000 + 400 + 2 =$
10. $4,000 + 600 + 70 + 4 =$
11. $300 + 50 + 2 =$
12. $5,000 + 200 + 60 + 8 =$
13. $2,000 + 100 + 90 =$
15. $300 + 80 + 4 =$

Down

1. $6,000 + 800 + 70 + 4 =$
2. $200 + 50 + 9 =$
4. $5,000 + 700 + 40 + 2 =$
5. $1,000 + 300 + 60 + 5 =$
7. $300 + 20 + 4 =$
8. $7,000 + 400 + 30 =$
9. $5,000 + 20 + 9 =$
14. $100 + 90 + 8 =$

Spring Cleaning

Find the place value of each underlined digit and circle the answer. To solve the riddle, write each circled letter in order on the answer lines.

1. 2<u>3</u>2,709
   C. thousands
   F. ten thousands
   R. hundred thousands

2. 763,6<u>1</u>0
   U. tens
   M. hundreds
   D. thousands

3. 78,06<u>6</u>
   R. ones
   B. tens
   L. hundreds

4. 7<u>5</u>7,386
   Y. thousands
   N. ten thousands
   A. hundred thousands

5. 99,7<u>2</u>6
   R. ones
   I. tens
   Z. hundreds

6. <u>1</u>36,644
   S. thousands
   E. ten thousands
   T. hundred thousands

7. 620,96<u>1</u>
   U. ones
   H. tens
   W. hundreds

8. 5<u>8</u>,085
   G. hundreds
   R. thousands
   S. ten thousands

9. 735,<u>9</u>04
   B. tens
   E. hundreds
   A. thousands

What does a bear put in his house?

HOME SWEET HOME

Answer: " ___ ___ ___ – ___ ___ ___ ___ ___ "

Name: _____

Number Word Search

**Identify the Roman numerals. Then, find each number word in the word search.
Words can be found down, across, and diagonally.**

```
O C L K U L U S E C P P O E G F P
O E S E M G X Q T W O O I G X V A
C Y V A F A B U C T I R S R Y Y S
Z X B X E F P M G I E B G L X I P
W R E M X I B N O G I E R S V K H
B F I V E F X R M N X P O A T R E
E G U R Y T F E B S E R Z T E N T
A X N X C Y D L I H A N F M L I J
V T S U C A D T W E N T Y R F O N
E R X E O G X Y X N I N E X I P T
T X X O V H S S K L N T X H F X Y
L A C S D E M L N K C H L Y T N R
A R A E D X N P A L K R F E E B O
D F V R I F P I K A W E S I E V Y
B R T G L G S N E B V E F O N Q C
C F R T Y R H Q O P X B H I I R K
C S O R T N H T N M W F P F X Y M
D J R U L O N E H U N D R E D T N
B O G D R Z O Q E S K H C U J Y Z
H S I X F Y L U O N G E Q M Z P X
```

1. VI _____ 2. L _____

3. VII _____ 4. I _____

5. III _____ 6. IV _____

7. C _____ 8. II _____

9. V _____ 10. X _____

11. VIII _____ 12. XV _____

13. XX _____ 14. IX _____

A Baker's "Dozin'"

Add to find each sum. Regroup if necessary. To solve the riddle, match the sums to the numbers below and write the correct letters on the answer lines. Hint: All of the letters will not be used, and some of the letters will be used more than once.

1.	97	2.	98	3.	71	4.	85	5.	19	6.	42
	+ 75		+ 33		+ 13		+ 62		+ 26		+ 26
	E		**I**		**A**		**L**		**R**		**W**

7.	59	8.	59	9.	277	10.	224	11.	415	12.	490
	+ 22		+ 91		+ 336		+ 365		+ 157		+ 337
	F		**H**		**S**		**Y**		**U**		**G**

13.	331	14.	603	15.	135	16.	378	17.	237	18.	146
	+ 151		+ 322		+ 586		+ 180		+ 507		+ 795
	P		**O**		**M**		**T**		**D**		**N**

Why did the lazy man want to work in a bakery?

Answer: ___ ___   ___ ___ ___   ___ ___ ___ ___ ___ ___
         150 172   68 84 613   150 925 482 131 941 827

___ ___   " ___ ___ ___   ___ " ___ ___ ___ ___ ___
558 925   147 925 84   81   84 45 925 572 941 744

Skater Math

Add to find each sum. Regroup if necessary. Then, complete the crossword puzzle.

Across

1. $728 + 147 =$
4. $847 + 105 =$
5. $222 + 99 =$
6. $488 + 208 =$
8. $388 + 881 =$
11. $655 + 239 =$
13. $337 + 139 =$
14. $86 + 28 =$
15. $581 + 176 =$
18. $495 + 177 =$

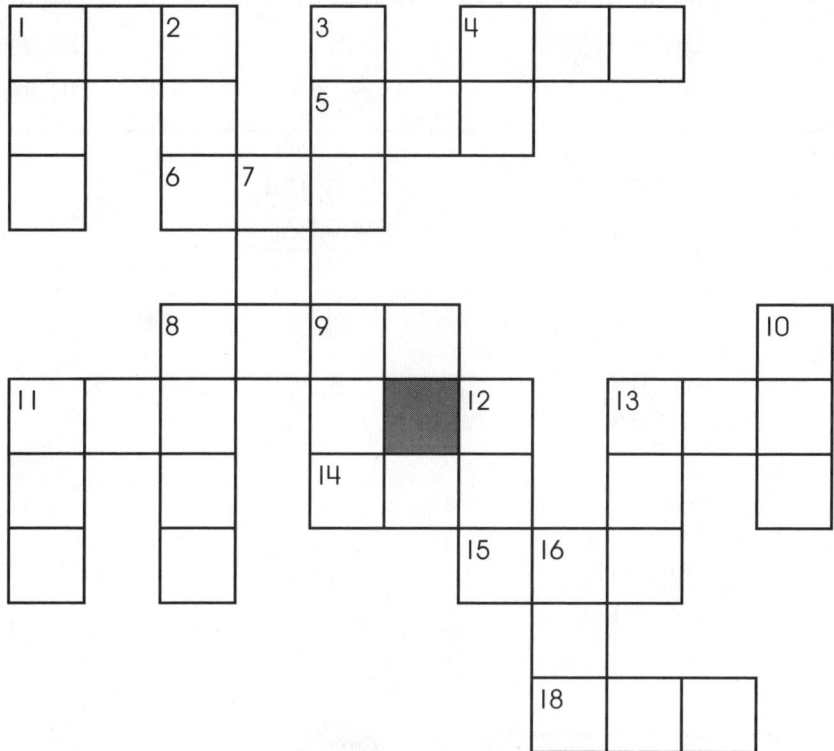

Down

1. $718 + 138 =$
2. $108 + 488 =$
3. $551 + 285 =$
4. $66 + 25 =$
7. $759 + 173 =$
8. $493 + 998 =$
9. $475 + 186 =$
10. $476 + 486 =$
11. $694 + 155 =$
12. $89 + 158 =$
13. $258 + 189 =$
16. $284 + 262 =$

Waterlogged

Add to find each sum. Regroup if necessary. Match each sum with the correct letter in the key. To solve the riddle, write the letters in order on the answer lines.

4,518 = N	7,185 = A	10,099 = O	10,427 = T
10,899 = P	11,603 = F	14,384 = C	15,970 = I

1. 1,431
    + 5,754

2. 5,324
    + 9,060

3. 4,386
    + 5,713

4. 3,402
    + 3,783

5. 3,144
    + 7,283

6. 8,704
    + 1,395

7. 3,378
    + 8,225

8. 1,115
    + 9,784

9. 2,174
    + 5,011

10. 8,958
    + 7,012

11. 1,515
    + 3,003

12. 9,046
    + 1,381

What kind of coat can be put on only when wet?

Answer: ____ " ____ ____ ____ " ____ ____ ____ ____ ____

"Sum" Crossword

Add to find each sum. Regroup if necessary. Then, complete the crossword puzzle.

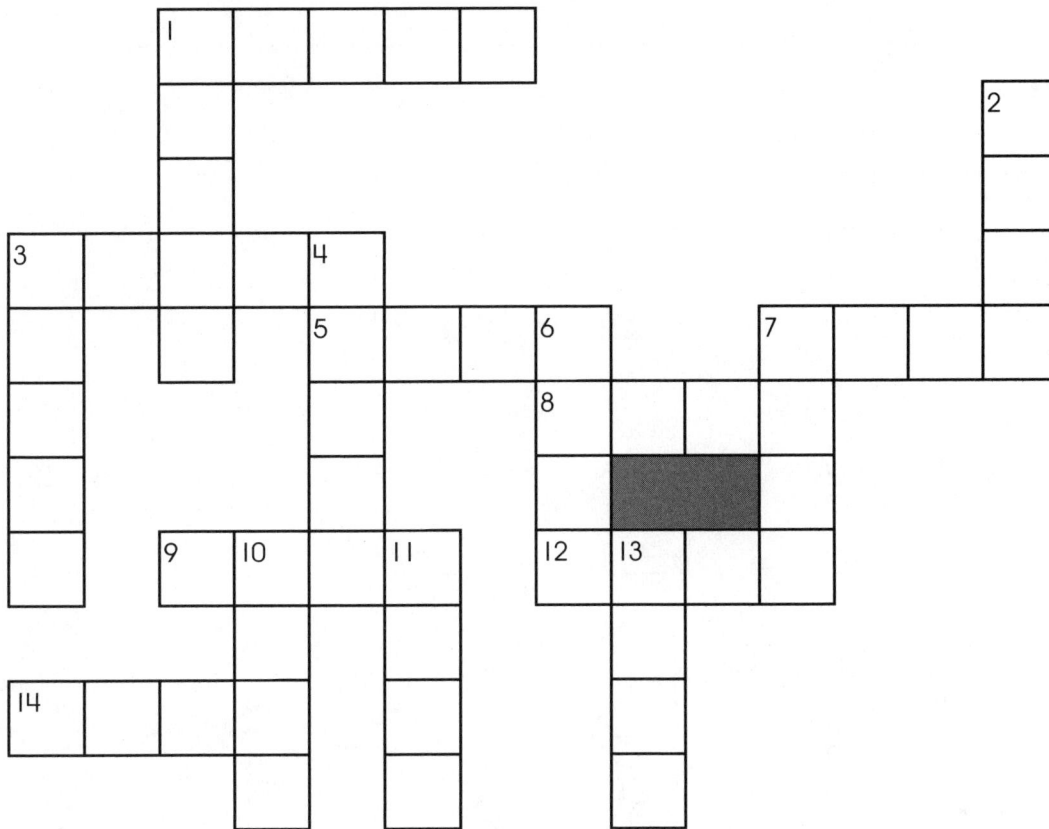

Across

1. $1{,}681 + 9{,}765 =$
3. $4{,}073 + 8{,}388 =$
5. $3{,}355 + 5{,}599 =$
7. $7{,}948 + 1{,}958 =$
8. $1{,}495 + 2{,}125 =$
9. $3{,}396 + 4{,}423 =$
12. $2{,}776 + 3{,}832 =$
14. $5{,}631 + 1{,}638 =$

Down

1. $9{,}485 + 4{,}055 =$
2. $3{,}905 + 1{,}911 =$
3. $1{,}905 + 8{,}974 =$
4. $8{,}770 + 9{,}951 =$
6. $2{,}249 + 2{,}147 =$
7. $7{,}188 + 1{,}910 =$
10. $1{,}809 + 6{,}484 =$
11. $3{,}864 + 5{,}920 =$
13. $4{,}463 + 2{,}184 =$

"Hare-Raising" Experience

Add to find each sum. Regroup if necessary. Match each sum with the correct letter in the key. To solve the riddle, write the letters in order on the answer lines.

271 = T	376 = I	516 = R	726 = F	899 = E
1,010 = N	1,110 = A	1,249 = O	1,461 = C	1,612 = H

1. 284
    32
 + 60

2. 874
    93
 + 43

3. 180
    51
 + 40

4. 641
   422
 + 549

5. 705
    96
 + 98

6. 864
   425
 + 323

7. 212
   491
 + 407

8. 432
    15
 + 69

9. 145
   345
 + 409

10. 123
    210
  + 393

11. 368
    830
  + 51

12. 126
    187
  + 203

13. 418
    458
  + 585

14. 623
    186
  + 90

Where do rabbits learn to fly?

Answer: ___ ___   ___ ___ ___ ___   " ___ ___ ___ ___ "

___ ___ ___ ___ ___

"Hoppy" Meal

Add to find each sum. Regroup if necessary. To solve the riddle, match the sums to the numbers below and write the correct letters on the answer lines. Hint: All of the letters will not be used, and some of the letters will be used more than once.

1.	$2.26 + $3.64 **U**	2.	$3.81 + $0.48 **D**	3.	$6.91 + $0.21 **B**	4.	$4.36 + $3.83 **G**	5.	$8.08 + $0.29 **C**
6.	$2.34 + $0.82 **T**	7.	$7.43 + $0.18 **H**	8.	$5.63 + $2.30 **R**	9.	$2.91 + $3.33 **Y**	10.	$3.96 + $3.61 **E**
11.	$4.57 + $2.31 **S**	12.	$2.09 + $6.36 **M**	13.	$4.92 + $4.40 **W**	14.	$6.53 + $0.39 **A**	15.	$6.15 + $1.92 **N**

Why are frogs so happy?

Answer: ___ ___ ___   ___ ___ ___ ___   ___ ___ ___ ___
$7.12 $7.57 $8.37 $6.92 $5.90 $6.88 $7.57 $3.16 $7.61 $7.57 $6.24

___ ___ ___   ___ ___ ___   ___ ___ ___ ___
$8.37 $6.92 $8.07 $7.57 $6.92 $3.16 $9.32 $7.61 $6.92 $3.16

"___ ___ ___ ___"   ___ ___ ___ ___
$7.12 $5.90 $8.19 $6.88 $3.16 $7.61 $7.57 $8.45

In Plain Sight

Add to find each sum. Regroup if necessary. To solve the riddle, match the sums to the numbers below and write the correct letters on the answer lines. Hint: Some of the letters will be used more than once.

1. 4.2
+ 3.2
O

2. 2.9
+ 3.9
S

3. 8.3
+ 1.6
U

4. 1.7
+ 3.9
Y

5. 1.5
+ 1.1
C

6. 2.5
+ 2.1
E

7. 3.5
+ 4.4
R

8. 2.5
+ 6.2
P

9. 2.2
+ 1.7
H

10. 2.5
+ 3.3
A

11. 3.7
+ 4.3
D

12. 2.8
+ 3.1
L

13. 5.9
+ 1.7
W

14. 2.8
+ 1.7
T

15. 5.8
+ 3.6
B

Why aren't leopards good at hide-and-seek?

Answer: ___ ___ ___ ___ ___ ___ ___   ___ ___ ___ ___
9.4 4.6 2.6 5.8 9.9 6.8 4.6   4.5 3.9 4.6 5.6

___ ___ ___   ___ ___ ___ ___ ___ ___
5.8 7.9 4.6   5.8 5.9 7.6 5.8 5.6 6.8

" ___ ___ ___ ___ ___ ___ ___ "
6.8 8.7 7.4 4.5 4.5 4.6 8.0

Fur Ball

Add to find each sum. Regroup if necessary. To solve the riddle, match the sums to the numbers below and write the correct letters on the answer lines. Hint: All of the letters will not be used, and some of the letters will be used more than once.

1. 1.13
    + 8.50
    F

2. 6.05
    + 8.49
    O

3. 3.23
    + 7.22
    N

4. 5.03
    + 4.33
    R

5. 2.41
    + 5.42
    D

6. 5.35
    + 8.59
    T

7. 7.62
    + 1.31
    G

8. 2.38
    + 4.58
    M

9. 5.34
    + 2.59
    U

10. 8.20
    + 1.36
    S

11. 9.76
    + 1.11
    I

12. 3.14
    + 2.55
    H

13. 6.35
    + 9.34
    A

14. 7.58
    + 1.34
    Y

15. 9.52
    + 7.23
    E

Who helped Cinderella's cat go to the ball?

Answer: ___ ___ ___ " ___ ___ ___ ___ ___ "
5.69 16.75 9.36   9.63 7.93 9.36 9.36 8.92

___ ___ ___ ___ ___ ___ ___ ___ ___
8.93 14.54 7.83 6.96 14.54 13.94 5.69 16.75 9.36

Story Time

Add to find each sum. Regroup if necessary.

1. Tanya has 276 fiction books and 187 nonfiction books. How many total books does she have?

2. Tanya's favorite book is *Traveling without Shoes*. The book has 214 pages of text and 122 pages of pictures. How many total pages are in the book?

3. Tanya's twin brother, Toby, has 348 fiction books and 109 nonfiction books. How many total books does he have?

4. Toby's favorite book is *Trees in the Breeze*. The book has 85 pages of text and 145 pages of pictures. How many total pages are in the book?

5. Tanya wants to buy two new books. One book costs $9.24, and the other costs $7.73. How much will the two books cost altogether?

6. Toby also wants to buy two new books. One book costs $7.87, and the other costs $5.21. How much will the two books cost altogether?

Deep Breath

What is gray, blue, and very big?

An elephant holding his breath!

Add to find each sum. Regroup if necessary.

1. Ellie, an African elephant, weighs 7,532 pounds. Her newborn calf weighs 189 pounds. How much do the elephants weigh together?

2. Ellie's friend, Santos, weighs 9,808 pounds. His brother, Dexter, weighs 9,267 pounds. How much do the elephants weigh together?

3. Last week, Ellie ate 1,835 pounds of vegetation, and Santos ate 2,060 pounds of vegetation. How many pounds of vegetation did the two elephants eat last week?

4. Last month, the elephants drank 3,208 gallons of water. This month, they drank 3,396. How many total gallons of water did they drink?

5. Ambika and Shanti are Asian elephants. Ambika weighs 7,379 pounds, and Shanti weighs 6,213 pounds. How much do the elephants weigh together?

6. Last year, Shanti gave birth to Kandula. At birth, Kandula weighed 268 pounds, and Shanti weighed 6,245 pounds. How much did the elephants weigh together?

Who's Calling?

Subtract to find each difference. Regroup if necessary. Match each difference with the correct letter in the key. To solve the riddle, write the letters in order on the answer lines.

7 = I	9 = E	14 = T	19 = A	26 = O	27 = C
36 = H	39 = L	47 = Y	60 = V	75 = R	82 = D

1. 53
    $- 39$

2. 83
    $- 47$

3. 64
    $- 55$

4. 85
    $- 38$

5. 65
    $- 29$

6. 75
    $- 56$

7. 71
    $- 11$

8. 67
    $- 58$

9. 41
    $- 14$

10. 80
    $- 54$

11. 65
    $- 26$

12. 72
    $- 33$

13. 47
    $- 28$

14. 91
    $- 16$

15. 22
    $- 15$

16. 93
    $- 11$

How are dogs like phones?

Answer: Because ____ ____ ____ ____   ____ ____ ____

" ____ ____ ____ ____ ____ " ____ ____

Super Subtraction

Subtract to find each difference. Regroup if necessary. Then, complete the crossword puzzle.

Across

1. $823 - 200 =$
3. $86 - 62 =$
6. $992 - 950 =$
8. $68 - 35 =$
9. $72 - 19 =$
11. $822 - 533 =$
13. $982 - 129 =$
15. $734 - 574 =$
17. $162 - 76 =$
18. $308 - 237 =$
19. $913 - 379 =$

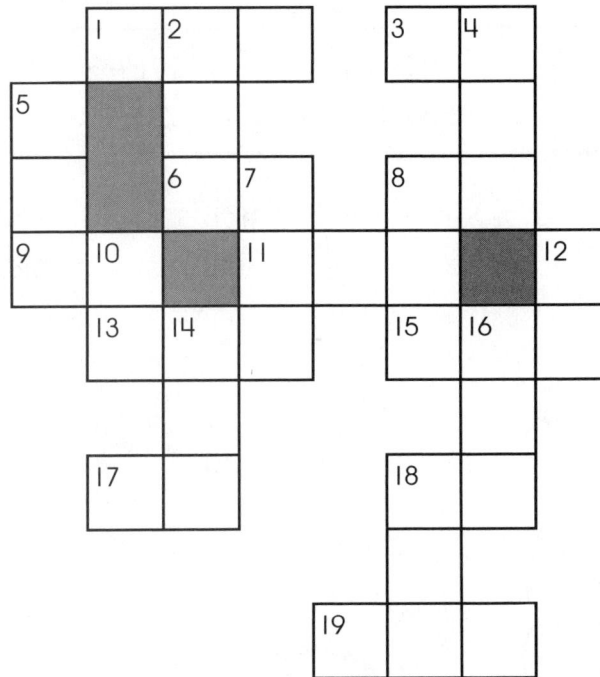

Down

2. $445 - 181 =$
4. $763 - 280 =$
5. $977 - 302 =$
7. $534 - 311 =$
8. $551 - 160 =$
10. $80 - 42 =$
12. $88 - 18 =$
14. $691 - 165 =$
16. $857 - 226 =$
18. $939 - 226 =$

Minty Fresh

Subtract to find each difference. Regroup if necessary. Match each difference with the correct letter in the key. To solve the riddle, write the letters in order on the answer lines.

78 = R	149 = N	191 = S	220 = P	248 = E
405 = T	589 = M	828 = X	865 = I	

1. $\begin{array}{r} 571 \\ -\ 323 \\ \hline \end{array}$
2. $\begin{array}{r} 949 \\ -\ 121 \\ \hline \end{array}$
3. $\begin{array}{r} 458 \\ -\ 238 \\ \hline \end{array}$
4. $\begin{array}{r} 588 \\ -\ 340 \\ \hline \end{array}$
5. $\begin{array}{r} 190 \\ -\ 112 \\ \hline \end{array}$
6. $\begin{array}{r} 992 \\ -\ 127 \\ \hline \end{array}$

7. $\begin{array}{r} 861 \\ -\ 272 \\ \hline \end{array}$
8. $\begin{array}{r} 989 \\ -\ 124 \\ \hline \end{array}$
9. $\begin{array}{r} 584 \\ -\ 435 \\ \hline \end{array}$
10. $\begin{array}{r} 728 \\ -\ 323 \\ \hline \end{array}$
11. $\begin{array}{r} 841 \\ -\ 650 \\ \hline \end{array}$

How do scientists freshen their breath?

Answer: With " ___ ___ ___ ___ ___ – ___ ___ ___ ___ ___ ___ "

Number Juggling

Subtract to find each difference. Regroup if necessary. Then, complete the crossword puzzle.

Across

2. 321 – 119 =

3. 493 – 248 =

4. 193 – 136 =

6. 278 – 226 =

8. 689 – 314 =

10. 419 – 233 =

12. 353 – 139 =

14. 835 – 217 =

16. 128 – 109 =

17. 473 – 109 =

19. 765 – 327 =

Down

1. 744 – 674 =

2. 361 – 336 =

3. 492 – 217 =

7. 312 – 290 =

8. 204 – 170 =

9. 925 – 362 =

10. 569 – 388 =

13. 282 – 146 =

18. 674 – 191 =

Traffic Jam

What do geese do in a traffic jam?

Subtract to find each difference. Regroup if necessary. Match the thousands digit in each difference with the correct letter in the key. To solve the riddle, write the letters in order on the answer lines.

1 = K	2 = O	3 = Y	4 = H	5 = T
6 = L	7 = E	8 = N	9 = A	

1. 5,657
    − 527

2. 5,393
    − 620

3. 7,581
    − 241

4. 3,599
    − 523

5. 5,314
    − 1,311

6. 6,818
    − 3,902

7. 8,680
    − 170

8. 2,157
    − 905

9. 9,478
    − 347

10. 8,123
    − 2,090

11. 3,498
    − 896

12. 8,635
    − 2,903

Answer: ____ ____ ____ ____ " ____ ____ ____ ____ ____ " ____ ____

Dancing to the Beat

Subtract to find each difference. Regroup if necessary. Then, complete the crossword puzzle.

Across

3. $7,019 - 5,741 =$

5. $1,394 - 423 =$

6. $7,170 - 1,528 =$

10. $3,772 - 3,432 =$

11. $358 - 230 =$

16. $9,946 - 9,142 =$

17. $9,404 - 5,473 =$

18. $3,355 - 3,108 =$

20. $4,226 - 101 =$

Down

1. $9,360 - 3,199 =$

2. $1,423 - 1,114 =$

4. $7,433 - 188 =$

7. $1,135 - 517 =$

8. $8,990 - 8,760 =$

12. $4,617 - 1,980 =$

13. $4,587 - 4,445 =$

14. $7,654 - 1,303 =$

19. $1,637 - 1,234 =$

Chow Down

Subtract to find each difference. Regroup if necessary. Match each difference with the correct letter in the key. To solve the riddle, write the numbers in order on the answer lines.

$1.17 = P	$1.24 = O	$1.36 = H	$2.40 = E
$4.29 = I	$5.33 = S	$5.37 = A	$9.03 = T

1. $12.69
   − $3.66

2. $12.55
   − $11.19

3. $12.38
   − $7.01

4. $10.70
   − $1.67

5. $8.46
   − $7.10

6. $6.82
   − $2.53

7. $11.46
   − $2.43

8. $9.76
   − $0.73

9. $8.29
   − $6.93

10. $12.03
   − $9.63

11. $13.45
   − $8.12

12. $9.34
   − $8.17

13. $5.04
   − $3.80

14. $16.73
   − $7.70

What did the hungry dalmatian say after eating?

Answer: ____ ____ ____ ____ ____ ____ ____ ____ ____

" ____ ____ ____ ____ "

I Can See Clearly

Subtract to find each difference. Regroup if necessary. To solve the riddle, match the differences to the numbers below and write the correct letters on the answer lines. Hint: Some of the letters will be used more than once.

1. 3.2 -1.2 **L**	2. 7.6 -6.8 **S**	3. 9.8 -5.1 **R**	4. 9.6 -5.6 **C**	5. 6.4 -5.8 **N**
6. 6.4 -2.7 **W**	7. 5.9 -4.6 **B**	8. 9.5 -2.2 **G**	9. 7.6 -2.3 **E**	10. 8.9 -1.5 **A**
11. 9.3 -8.2 **I**	12. 7.7 -6.1 **T**	13. 9.3 -6.3 **D**	14. 9.9 -6.6 **U**	15. 8.2 -6.7 **O**

How do you know that carrots are good for your eyesight?

Answer: ___ ___ ___ ___ ___ ___ ___
1.3 5.3 4.0 7.4 3.3 0.8 5.3

___ ___ ___ ___ ___ ___ ___   ___ ___   ___ ___ ___
4.7 7.4 1.3 1.3 1.1 1.6 0.8   3.0 1.5   0.6 1.5 1.6

___ ___ ___ ___   ___ ___ ___ ___ ___ ___ ___
3.7 5.3 7.4 4.7   7.3 2.0 7.4 0.8 0.8 5.3 0.8

Full Plate

Subtract to find each difference. Regroup if necessary. To solve the riddle, match the differences to the numbers below and write the correct letters on the answer lines. Hint: All of the letters will not be used, and some of the letters will be used more than once.

1. 2.21
    − 0.40
    D

2. 3.73
    − 1.29
    G

3. 5.56
    − 2.82
    Y

4. 8.96
    − 6.13
    F

5. 0.50
    − 0.12
    C

6. 8.41
    − 0.92
    O

7. 6.76
    − 0.55
    A

8. 9.86
    − 6.84
    R

9. 6.87
    − 2.04
    B

10. 3.59
    − 1.98
    H

11. 3.40
    − 0.68
    T

12. 4.75
    − 1.87
    S

13. 9.97
    − 6.86
    N

14. 5.49
    − 0.30
    U

15. 7.28
    − 6.12
    E

Why did the customer in the restaurant keep laughing?

Answer: ___ ___ ___ ___ ___ ___ ___   ___ ___ ___
4.83 1.16 0.38 6.21 5.19 2.88 1.16   1.61 1.16 3.02

___ ___ ___ ___   ___ ___ ___ ___ ___ ___   " ___ ___ ___ ___ ___ "
2.83 7.49 7.49 1.81   2.72 6.21 2.88 2.72 1.16 1.81   2.83 5.19 3.11 3.11 2.74

Pack Your Bags

Subtract to find each difference. Regroup if necessary.

1. A Jupiter Jet can carry 440 passengers. On a recent trip, a Jupiter Jet carried 376 passengers. How many seats were empty?

2. Juanita has $84.00. She uses $29.00 to buy sandals for a trip to the beach. How much money does she have left?

3. Tyler bought a fishing pole for $34.29. He had a coupon that saved him $4.30. How much did the fishing pole cost after using the coupon?

4. Meredith started hiking at an elevation of 1,233 feet. She hiked until she reached 3,896 feet. How far up the mountain did she hike?

5. Last summer, the local ice cream store sold 7,688 hot fudge sundaes, 5,604 chocolate sundaes, and 3,592 strawberry sundaes.

   A. How many more hot fudge sundaes were sold than chocolate sundaes?

   B. How many more hot fudge sundaes were sold than strawberry sundaes?

6. On Saturday, 2,352 men, 3,851 women, and 3,433 children were in the stands at a Portland Ponies game.

   A. How many more women attended than men?

   B. How many more women attended than children?

"Ship-Shop"

Subtract to find each difference. Regroup if necessary.

1. Mandy wants to buy a pair of binoculars that cost $39.45. She has $24.00. How much more money does she need?

2. Luke needs 415 balloons for a party. He has 166 balloons. How many more balloons does he need to buy?

3. Nellie bought a new camera for $92.19. She received a discount of $25.00. How much did the camera cost after the discount?

4. Patrick bought a mixed bag of peanuts and raisins. If the bag contains 2,017 total pieces and 984 of them are raisins, how many peanuts are in the bag?

5. Last month, Mrs. Lebeau spent $68.35 on supplies and $35.60 on lunch. This month, she spent $82.73 on supplies and $53.90 for lunch.

    A. How much more did she spend on supplies this month than last month?

    B. How much more did she spend on lunch this month than last month?

6. Ryan is selling fruit at Stanton's Fruit Stand. On Monday, he started with 635 apples and 320 peaches. On Friday, he had 428 apples and 189 peaches left.

    A. How many apples did Ryan sell?

    B. How many peaches did Ryan sell?

Name: _____

Rainy Forecast

Multiply to find each product. To solve the riddle, match the products to the numbers below and write the correct letters on the answer lines. Hint: All of the letters will not be used, and some of the letters will be used more than once.

1. $\begin{array}{r} 10 \\ \times\ 2 \\ \hline \end{array}$
D

2. $\begin{array}{r} 3 \\ \times\ 8 \\ \hline \end{array}$
I

3. $\begin{array}{r} 0 \\ \times\ 4 \\ \hline \end{array}$
F

4. $\begin{array}{r} 6 \\ \times\ 7 \\ \hline \end{array}$
C

5. $\begin{array}{r} 10 \\ \times\ 3 \\ \hline \end{array}$
O

6. $\begin{array}{r} 2 \\ \times\ 7 \\ \hline \end{array}$
A

7. $\begin{array}{r} 3 \\ \times\ 6 \\ \hline \end{array}$
L

8. $\begin{array}{r} 6 \\ \times\ 6 \\ \hline \end{array}$
B

9. $\begin{array}{r} 9 \\ \times\ 3 \\ \hline \end{array}$
H

10. $\begin{array}{r} 3 \\ \times\ 2 \\ \hline \end{array}$
T

11. $\begin{array}{r} 4 \\ \times\ 4 \\ \hline \end{array}$
S

12. $\begin{array}{r} 8 \\ \times\ 5 \\ \hline \end{array}$
N

13. $\begin{array}{r} 4 \\ \times\ 1 \\ \hline \end{array}$
U

14. $\begin{array}{r} 7 \\ \times\ 3 \\ \hline \end{array}$
E

15. $\begin{array}{r} 4 \\ \times\ 3 \\ \hline \end{array}$
R

How did the skeleton know that it was going to rain?

Answer: ___ ___   ___ ___ ___ ___ ___   ___ ___ ___ ___
27   21   42   30   4   18   20   0   21   21   18

       " ___   "
___ ___   ___ ___   ___ ___ ___   ___ ___ ___ ___ ___
24   6   24   40   27   24   16   36   30   40   21   16

Turtle Talk

Multiply to find each product. Match each product with the correct letter in the key. To solve the riddle, write the letters in order on the answer lines.

24 = H	32 = P	36 = E	40 = S	56 = N
60 = L	70 = W	72 = O	77 = I	144 = T

1. $7 \times 10 =$ 2. $11 \times 7 =$ 3. $12 \times 12 =$ 4. $2 \times 12 =$

5. $8 \times 5 =$ 6. $8 \times 3 =$ 7. $9 \times 4 =$ 8. $10 \times 6 =$

9. $12 \times 5 =$ 10. $8 \times 4 =$ 11. $12 \times 2 =$ 12. $8 \times 9 =$

13. $8 \times 7 =$ 14. $12 \times 3 =$ 15. $10 \times 4 =$

> How do turtles communicate with each other?

Answer: ___ ___ ___ ___   " ___ ___ ___ ___ ___ "

___ ___ ___ ___ ___

Wiggle Room

Multiply to find each product. To solve the riddle, match the products to the numbers below and write the correct letters on the answer lines. Hint: All of the letters will not be used, and some of the letters will be used more than once.

1.	2.	3.	4.	5.	6.
14 × 2 **E**	43 × 3 **O**	33 × 2 **S**	90 × 5 **A**	35 × 1 **H**	50 × 6 **V**

7.	8.	9.	10.	11.	12.
31 × 4 **I**	45 × 1 **T**	21 × 4 **R**	83 × 3 **C**	21 × 5 **B**	33 × 3 **W**

13.	14.	15.	16.	17.	18.
75 × 1 **Y**	51 × 2 **G**	32 × 4 **M**	52 × 4 **U**	61 × 5 **N**	72 × 3 **L**

Speech bubble: What did the mother worm say to the little worm that was late?

Answer: __ __ __ __ __ " __ __ __ __ __ __ "
     99   35   28   84   28   124   305   28   450   84   45   35

__ __ __ __   __ __ __   __ __ __ __?
35   450   300   28   75   129   208   105   28   28   305

Name: _____

Flying South

Multiply to find each product. To solve the riddle, match the products to the numbers below and write the correct letters on the answer lines. Hint: All of the letters will not be used, and some of the letters will be used more than once.

1. $\begin{array}{r} 27 \\ \times\ 4 \\ \hline \end{array}$
    L

2. $\begin{array}{r} 14 \\ \times\ 3 \\ \hline \end{array}$
    W

3. $\begin{array}{r} 18 \\ \times\ 5 \\ \hline \end{array}$
    C

4. $\begin{array}{r} 28 \\ \times\ 5 \\ \hline \end{array}$
    O

5. $\begin{array}{r} 29 \\ \times\ 2 \\ \hline \end{array}$
    B

6. $\begin{array}{r} 16 \\ \times\ 6 \\ \hline \end{array}$
    I

7. $\begin{array}{r} 25 \\ \times\ 7 \\ \hline \end{array}$
    N

8. $\begin{array}{r} 27 \\ \times\ 3 \\ \hline \end{array}$
    T

9. $\begin{array}{r} 19 \\ \times\ 5 \\ \hline \end{array}$
    E

10. $\begin{array}{r} 23 \\ \times\ 4 \\ \hline \end{array}$
    K

11. $\begin{array}{r} 28 \\ \times\ 3 \\ \hline \end{array}$
    U

12. $\begin{array}{r} 22 \\ \times\ 6 \\ \hline \end{array}$
    F

13. $\begin{array}{r} 36 \\ \times\ 2 \\ \hline \end{array}$
    R

14. $\begin{array}{r} 14 \\ \times\ 5 \\ \hline \end{array}$
    A

15. $\begin{array}{r} 26 \\ \times\ 2 \\ \hline \end{array}$
    S

Why do birds fly south?

Answer: _____

58 95 90 70 84 52 95   96 81   96 52

81 140 140   132 70 72   81 140   42 70 108 92

Worth Their Weight

Multiply to find each product. To solve the riddle, match the products to the numbers below and write the correct letters on the answer lines. Hint: All of the letters will not be used, and some of the letters will be used more than once.

1. $\begin{array}{r} 47 \\ \times\ 2 \\ \hline \end{array}$ **L**   2. $\begin{array}{r} 47 \\ \times\ 7 \\ \hline \end{array}$ **W**   3. $\begin{array}{r} 59 \\ \times\ 3 \\ \hline \end{array}$ **C**   4. $\begin{array}{r} 35 \\ \times\ 6 \\ \hline \end{array}$ **P**   5. $\begin{array}{r} 24 \\ \times\ 4 \\ \hline \end{array}$ **O**   6. $\begin{array}{r} 36 \\ \times\ 6 \\ \hline \end{array}$ **B**

7. $\begin{array}{r} 17 \\ \times\ 5 \\ \hline \end{array}$ **I**   8. $\begin{array}{r} 13 \\ \times\ 8 \\ \hline \end{array}$ **T**   9. $\begin{array}{r} 74 \\ \times\ 8 \\ \hline \end{array}$ **E**   10. $\begin{array}{r} 37 \\ \times\ 9 \\ \hline \end{array}$ **N**   11. $\begin{array}{r} 86 \\ \times\ 3 \\ \hline \end{array}$ **V**   12. $\begin{array}{r} 27 \\ \times\ 7 \\ \hline \end{array}$ **F**

13. $\begin{array}{r} 84 \\ \times\ 4 \\ \hline \end{array}$ **R**   14. $\begin{array}{r} 56 \\ \times\ 4 \\ \hline \end{array}$ **A**   15. $\begin{array}{r} 37 \\ \times\ 6 \\ \hline \end{array}$ **S**   16. $\begin{array}{r} 47 \\ \times\ 8 \\ \hline \end{array}$ **U**   17. $\begin{array}{r} 29 \\ \times\ 9 \\ \hline \end{array}$ **H**   18. $\begin{array}{r} 73 \\ \times\ 4 \\ \hline \end{array}$ **M**

Why is it so easy to weigh fish?

Answer: ___ ___ ___ ___ ___ ___ ___   ___ ___ ___ ___
216   592   177   224   376   222   592   189   85   222   261

___ ___ ___ ___   ___ ___ ___ ___ ___   ___ ___ ___
261   224   258   592   104   261   592   85   336   96   329   333

" ___ ___ ___ ___ ___ ___ "
222   177   224   94   592   222

Name: _____

Holding the Key

What kind of keys do kids like to carry?

"Coo-kies!"

Use the information below to find each product.

Marshmallow Puffs = 5 cookies in each box
Mighty Mints = 6 cookies in each box
Gingersnap Delights = 7 cookies in each box
Low-Fat Fudge Bites = 8 cookies in each box

1. Jermaine bought 4 boxes of Low-Fat Fudge Bites. How many Low-Fat Fudge Bites does he have?

2. Kayla bought 5 boxes of Gingersnap Delights. How many Gingersnap Delights does she have?

3. Owen bought 3 boxes of Marshmallow Puffs. How many Marshmallow Puffs does he have?

4. Isabelle bought 7 boxes of Mighty Mints. How many Mighty Mints does she have?

5. Louis sold 8 boxes of Marshmallow Puffs and 6 boxes of Gingersnap Delights. How many cookies of each type did he sell?

   A. _____ Marshmallow Puffs

   B. _____ Gingersnap Delights

6. Each type of cookie is shipped in a case with 9 boxes inside. How many total cookies are in each case?

   A. _____ Marshmallow Puffs

   B. _____ Mighty Mints

   C. _____ Gingersnap Delights

   D. _____ Low-Fat Fudge Bites

Name: _____

"A-Doorable" Disguise

Review each problem. Cross out the incorrect problems. To solve the riddle, write the remaining letters in order on the answer lines.

1. $20 \div 4 = 5$ **W**
2. $21 \div 3 = 6$ **S**
3. $2 \div 1 = 2$ **H**
4. $27 \div 3 = 9$ **E**
5. $4 \div 2 = 8$ **R**
6. $18 \div 2 = 9$ **N**
7. $12 \div 4 = 4$ **J**
8. $40 \div 5 = 7$ **S**
9. $9 \div 1 = 9$ **I**
10. $10 \div 2 = 6$ **L**
11. $32 \div 4 = 8$ **T**
12. $8 \div 2 = 4$ **I**
13. $3 \div 2 = 3$ **E**
14. $45 \div 6 = 9$ **R**
15. $7 \div 1 = 7$ **S**
16. $15 \div 5 = 2$ **K**
17. $24 \div 3 = 8$ **A**
18. $24 \div 5 = 6$ **P**
19. $14 \div 2 = 7$ **J**
20. $12 \div 3 = 5$ **N**
21. $35 \div 5 = 8$ **Y**
22. $18 \div 3 = 6$ **A**
23. $28 \div 4 = 8$ **L**
24. $6 \div 3 = 2$ **R**

When is a door not a door?

Answer: ____ ____ ____ ____ ____ ____ "____ - ____ ____ ____"

Parallel Parking

Divide to find each quotient. Match each quotient with the correct letter in the key. To solve the riddle, write the letters in order on the answer lines.

1 = R	2 = O	3 = A	4 = E	5 = P	6 = N
7 = T	8 = K	9 = I	10 = S	11 = G	12 = M

1. $7\overline{)21}$
2. $9\overline{)63}$
3. $8\overline{)40}$
4. $12\overline{)36}$

5. $8\overline{)8}$
6. $10\overline{)80}$
7. $7\overline{)63}$
8. $12\overline{)72}$

9. $11\overline{)121}$
10. $9\overline{)108}$
11. $8\overline{)32}$
12. $12\overline{)84}$

13. $9\overline{)36}$
14. $9\overline{)18}$
15. $12\overline{)12}$
16. $11\overline{)110}$

Where do astronauts park their spacecraft?

Answer: ___ ___   ___ ___ ___ ___ ___

" ___ ___ ___ ___ ___ ___ ___ "

Cash Cow

Use the information below to find each quotient.

Tomato seeds = 9 seeds per packet
Cabbage seeds = 8 seeds per packet
Squash seeds = 7 seeds per packet
Pumpkin seeds = 6 seeds per packet

1. Emma wants to grow 40 cabbage plants. How many packets of cabbage seeds does she need to buy?

2. Travis wants to grow 36 tomato plants. How many packets of tomato seeds does he need to buy?

3. Yvonne planted 32 cabbage seeds, 35 squash seeds, and 30 pumpkin seeds.

   A. How many packets of cabbage seeds did she buy?

   B. How many packets of squash seeds did she buy?

   C. How many packets of pumpkin seeds did she buy?

4. Quinn planted 54 tomato seeds, 64 cabbage seeds, and 63 squash seeds.

   A. How many packets of tomato seeds did he buy?

   B. How many packets of cabbage seeds did he buy?

   C. How many packets of squash seeds did he buy?

Family Tree

Use each set of numbers to make two multiplication problems and two division problems.

1.   4, 6, 24   _____ _____ _____ _____

2.   6, 7, 42   _____ _____ _____ _____

3.   4, 8, 32   _____ _____ _____ _____

4.   5, 9, 45   _____ _____ _____ _____

5.   7, 9, 63   _____ _____ _____ _____

6.   5, 7, 35   _____ _____ _____ _____

7.   7, 8, 56   _____ _____ _____ _____

8.   6, 8, 48   _____ _____ _____ _____

9.   8, 9, 72   _____ _____ _____ _____

10. 5, 8, 40   _____ _____ _____ _____

Riddle Me This

Identify each fraction. Draw a line to match each fraction in column 1 to the equivalent fraction in column 2. To solve the riddle, write the letters in column 2 in order on the answer lines.

Column 1

1.
2.
3.
4.
5.
6.
7.
8.
9.
10.

Column 2

$\frac{5}{6}$ **E**

$\frac{1}{10}$ **A**

$\frac{1}{6}$ **E**

$\frac{3}{4}$ **L**

$\frac{1}{4}$ **H**

$\frac{1}{3}$ **E**

$\frac{1}{2}$ **O**

$\frac{2}{5}$ **T**

$\frac{3}{5}$ **N**

$\frac{4}{5}$ **P**

What never asks questions but must always be answered?

Answer: ____   ____ ____ ____ ____ ____ ____ ____ ____ ____

Name: _____

"Bee" Healthy

Identify each fraction. Use >, <, or = to compare each pair of fractions. Circle the letter next to the greater fraction. If the fractions are equal, circle both letters. To solve the riddle, write the circled letters in order on the answer lines.

1. V ◯ S
   ___

2. R ◯ I
   ___

3. T ◯ A
   ___

4. N ◯ M
   ___

5. I ◯ U
   ___

6. N ◯ B
   ___

7. R ◯ E
   ___

8. E ◯ S
   ___

What bee is good for your health?

Answer: ___ ___ ___ ___ ___ " ___ ___ ___ "

42

Name: _____

Three Feet

Identify each fraction. Draw a line to match each fraction in column 1 to the equivalent fraction in column 2. To solve the riddle, write the letters in column 2 in order on the answer lines.

Column 1	**Column 2**

1. 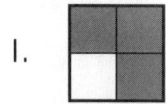   ● ● ○   **I**

2. 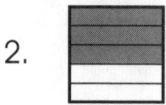      **R**

3. 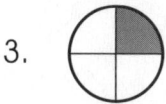      **S**

4. 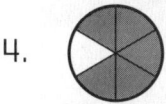   ● ● ● ○ ○   **A**

5. 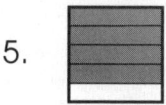   ● ● ● ● ● ○   **D**

6. 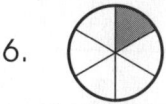   ● ○ ○ ○ ○ ○   **T**

7. 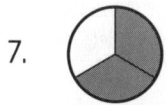   ● ○ ○ ○ ○ ○ ○   **K**

8. 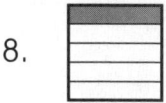      **Y**

9. 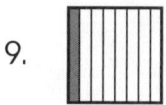      **C**

What has one foot on each side and one in the middle?

Answer: A   ___ ___ ___ ___ ___ ___ ___ ___ ___

On Schedule

Speech bubbles: "What makes a calendar seem so friendly?" · "It has so many "dates.""

Jaelynn needs to fill in her appointment calendar. Use the calendar and the information provided to find the date for each event.

MAY						
Sunday	Monday	Tuesday	Wednesday	Thursday	Friday	Saturday
	1	2	3	4	5	6
7	8	9	10	11	12	13
14	15	16	17	18	19	20
21	22	23	24	25	26	27
28	29	30	31			

1. Today is May 17. The softball game was 12 days earlier. _____

2. Today is May 27. The dentist appointment was 10 days earlier. _____

3. Today is May 14. Going shopping with Maggie in 11 days. _____

4. Today is May 22. Going to Florida in 9 days. _____

5. Today is May 9. The piano lesson was 1 week earlier. _____

6. Today is May 16. Dinner with Douglas was 5 days earlier. _____

7. Today is May 10. Veterinarian appointment for Sparkles is in two weeks.

_____

8. Today is May 21. Went horseback riding 7 days earlier. _____

Early Risers

What time do frogs and toads wake up?

Zzzz

At the "croak" of dawn!

Identify each time. Draw a line to match each analog clock to the digital clock that shows the same time.

1.

2.

3.

4.

5.

9:15

1:50

4:45

2:20

8:10

Name: _____

Outer Space

Draw a line to match each time in column 1 to the elapsed time in column 2. To solve the riddle, write the letters in column 2 in order on the answer lines.

Column 1

1.   1:10 A.M. to 1:45 A.M.
2.   11:05 A.M. to 2:00 P.M.
3.   7:35 P.M. to 8:45 P.M.
4.   10:50 A.M. to 12:30 P.M.
5.   8:30 P.M. to midnight
6.   2:30 P.M. to 7:45 P.M.
7.   5:00 P.M. to 5:45 P.M.
8.   4:10 A.M. to 7:50 A.M.
9.   6:25 P.M. to 12:25 A.M.
10. 3:25 P.M. to 6:30 P.M.
11. 9:55 A.M. to 2:05 P.M.
12. 1:40 P.M. to 3:55 P.M.

Column 2

3 hours, 30 minutes   **D**

2 hours, 15 minutes   **E**

1 hour, 10 minutes   **E**

2 hours, 55 minutes   **N**

1 hour, 40 minutes   **E**

6 hours   **P**

3 hours, 40 minutes   **S**

35 minutes   **I**

45 minutes   **Y**

3 hours, 5 minutes   **A**

4 hours, 10 minutes   **C**

5 hours, 15 minutes   **M**

> What did one planet say to the other planet?

Answer: ____ ____ ____ ____ ____ "____ ____ ____ ____"

© Carson-Dellosa • CD-104286

Funny Money

Circle the best unit of length for each problem. To solve the riddle, write each circled letter in order on the answer lines.

1. Distance between two cities
   - R. Meters
   - D. Kilometers

2. Length of a car
   - A. Centimeters
   - O. Meters

3. Length of a caterpillar
   - L. Centimeters
   - S. Meters

4. Length of the Mississippi River
   - E. Meters
   - L. Kilometers

5. Width of a room
   - A. Meters
   - N. Kilometers

6. Height of a strawberry
   - R. Centimeters
   - T. Meters

7. Distance between the earth and the moon
   - A. Meters
   - S. Kilometers

8. Height of a robin
   - S. Inches
   - R. Feet

9. Length of a pencil
   - C. Inches
   - O. Feet

10. Height of a giraffe
    - L. Inches
    - E. Feet

11. Distance a plane flies in one hour
    - A. Feet
    - N. Miles

12. Length of your bed
    - B. Inches
    - T. Feet

13. Height of a skyscraper
    - S. Feet
    - L. Miles

What do you get when you cross a bank with a skunk?

Answer:

____ ____ ____ ____ ____ ____ ____ and " ____ ____ ____ ____ ____ "

Nosing Around

Read the rulers below to find the length of each bar.

1. 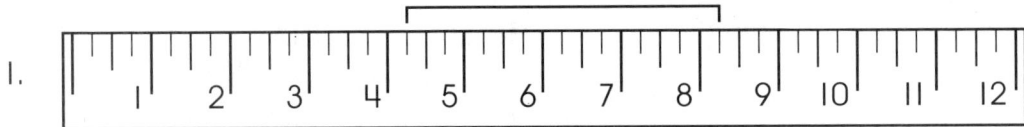 _____ in.

2. 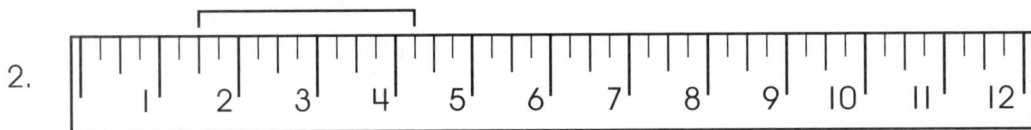 _____ in.

3. 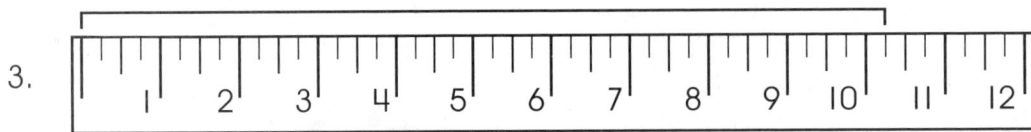 _____ in.

4. 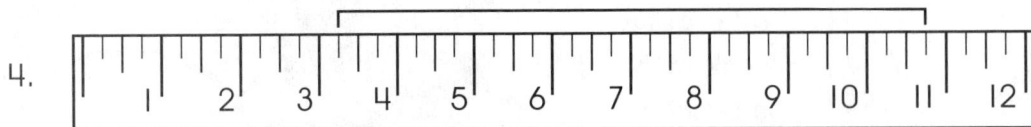 _____ in.

5. 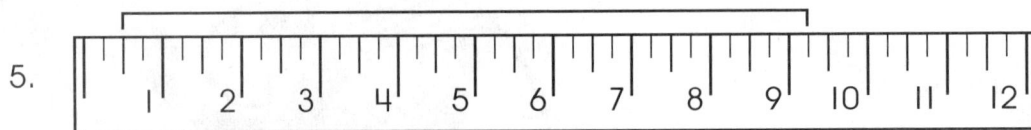 _____ in.

6. 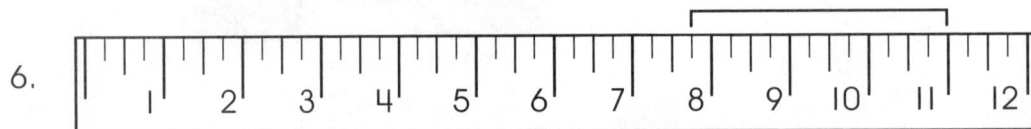 _____ in.

Stay Tuned

Find each object. Then, use a ruler to measure each object to the nearest millimeter.

1. An eraser _____
2. A paper clip _____
3. A piece of chalk _____
4. A tack _____
5. A magnet _____
6. A coin _____

Find each object. Then, use a ruler to measure each object to the nearest centimeter.

7. An unsharpened pencil _____
8. A sharpened pencil _____
9. A book _____
10. A sheet of paper _____
11. A stapler _____
12. A calculator _____
13. A bottle of glue _____
14. A pair of scissors _____
15. Your shoe _____
16. Your hand _____

Shiny Smile

Use > or < to compare each pair of amounts. Circle the letter next to the larger amount. To solve the riddle, write the circled letters in order on the answer lines. Use the information provided for help.

2 cups = 1 pint	2 pints = 1 quart	4 quarts = 1 gallon

1.	**T**	5 cups	◯	1 pint **A**
2.	**L**	1 pint	◯	1 quart **H**
3.	**E**	2 gallons	◯	3 quarts **D**
4.	**Y**	2 pints	◯	1 cup **S**
5.	**K**	2 pints	◯	5 cups **H**
6.	**A**	5 quarts	◯	1 gallon **E**
7.	**U**	2 quarts	◯	6 pints **V**
8.	**E**	7 cups	◯	1 quart **O**
9.	**C**	2 quarts	◯	1 gallon **B**
10.	**U**	1 gallon	◯	4 pints **V**
11.	**D**	1 quart	◯	5 cups **C**
12.	**J**	3 pints	◯	1 gallon **K**
13.	**T**	20 cups	◯	1 gallon **S**
14.	**E**	2 pints	◯	3 cups **O**
15.	**A**	2 cups	◯	2 pints **E**
16.	**S**	3 quarts	◯	1 gallon **T**
17.	**R**	3 quarts	◯	2 gallons **H**

Why do male deer need braces?

Answer: Because   ___ ___ ___ ___   ___ ___ ___

" ___ ___ ___ ___ "   ___ ___ ___

Summertime

Which days in the summer are the hottest?

"Sun-days!"

Read each thermometer. Write the temperatures for each thermometer.

1. 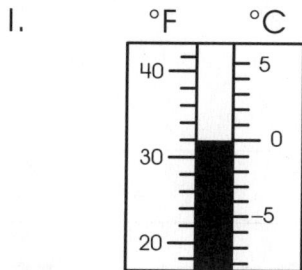   _____ °F   _____ °C

2. 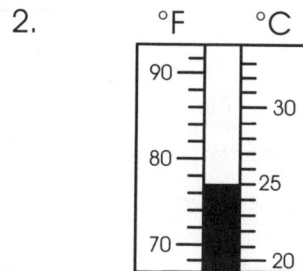   _____ °F   _____ °C

3. 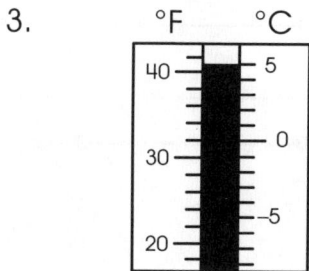   _____ °F   _____ °C

4. 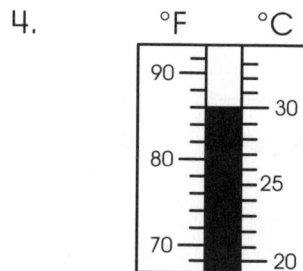   _____ °F   _____ °C

5. 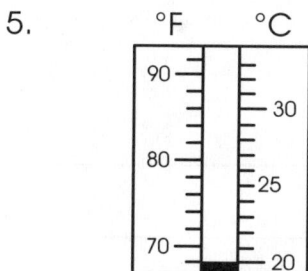   _____ °F   _____ °C

6. 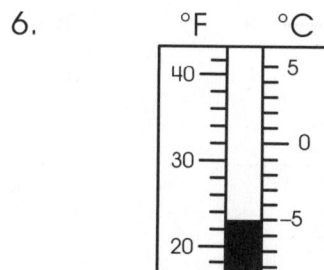   _____ °F   _____ °C

Running in Circles

Identify each figure as a point, ray, line, or line segment. Then, name each figure.

1. • S

_____

_____

2.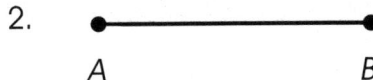
A   B

_____

_____

3. • M

_____

_____

4.
L   M

_____

_____

5.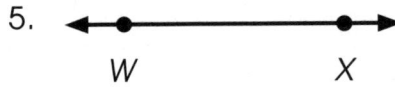
W   X

_____

_____

6.
Q   R

_____

_____

7.
J   K

_____

_____

8. • F

_____

_____

9.
C   D

_____

_____

10.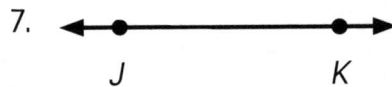
H   I

_____

_____

11.
U   V

_____

_____

12. • Y

_____

_____

The Right Angle

Oswald Obtuse, Rashad Right, and Allie Acute are trying to get home. They can only travel on paths with angles that match their own last names. Use this information and colorful pencils to help each person get home.

Polygon Puzzle

Use the clues to complete the crossword puzzle.

hexagon	octagon	pentagon	polygon
rectangle	square	trapezoid	triangle

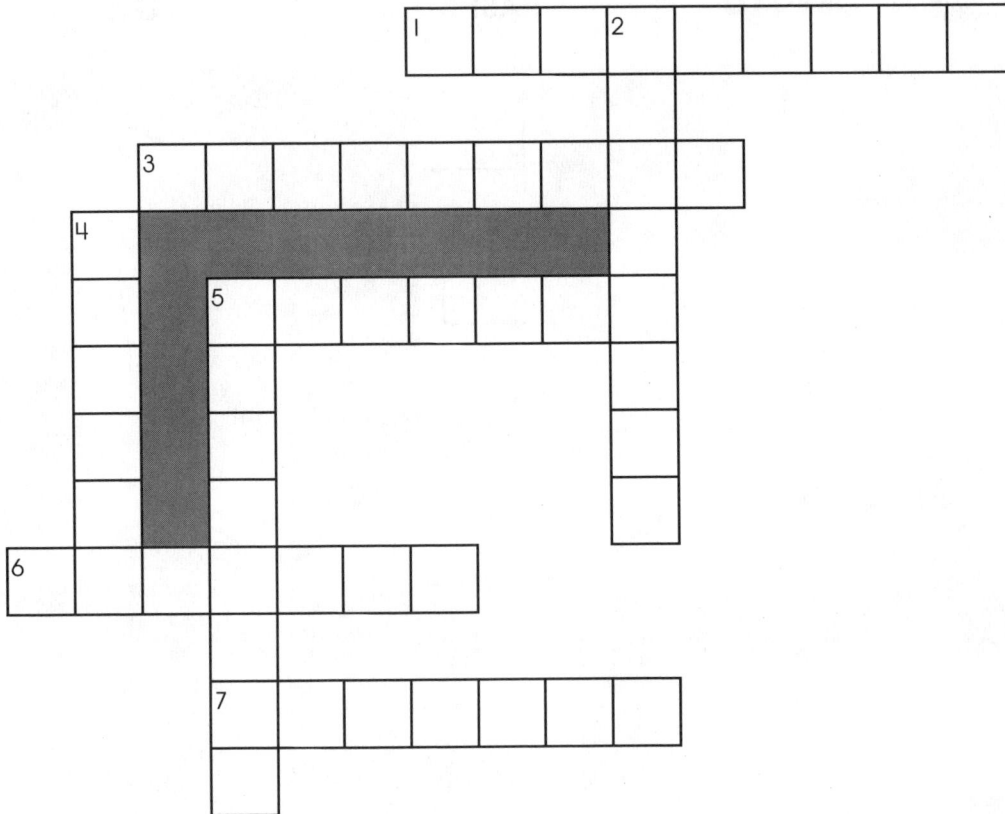

Across

1. A four-sided polygon with opposite sides that are equal and parallel
3. A four-sided polygon with only one pair of parallel sides
5. Line segments joined to form a closed figure
6. A six-sided polygon
7. An eight-sided polygon

Down

2. A three-sided polygon
4. A four-sided polygon with four equal sides and opposite sides that are parallel
5. A five-sided polygon

Triangle Treats

Identify each triangle as acute, right, or obtuse. Write the letters in the acute triangles in order to solve Riddle 1. Write the letters in the obtuse triangles in order to solve Riddle 2. Write the letters in the right triangles in order to solve Riddle 3.

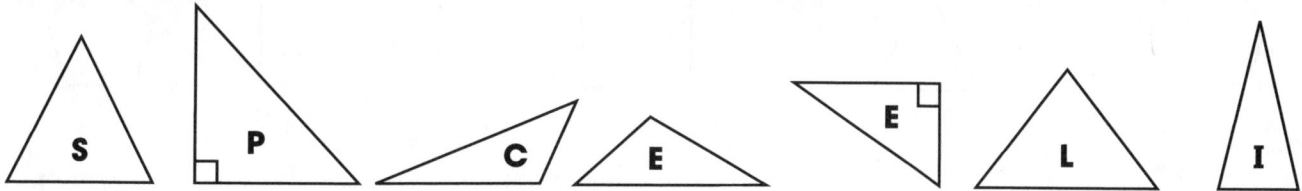

_____ _____ _____ _____ _____ _____ _____

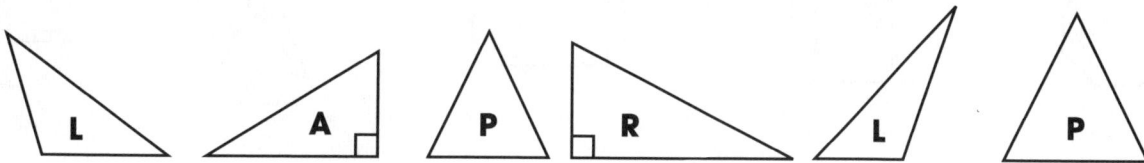

_____ _____ _____ _____ _____ _____

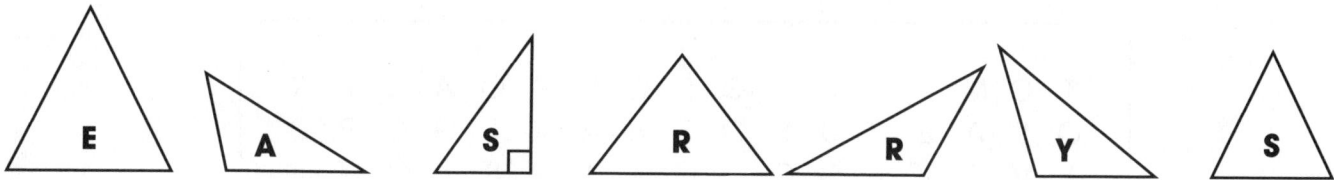

_____ _____ _____ _____ _____ _____ _____

Riddle 1: What kind of shoes are made from banana peels?

   Answer: " ___ ___ ___ ___ ___ ___ ___ "

Riddle 2: What vegetable might you find in your basement?

   Answer: " ___ ___ ___ ___ ___ ___ – ___ "

Riddle 3: What are twins' favorite fruit?

   Answer: " ___ ___ ___ ___ ___ "

Figure It Out

Identify each figure. Then, find each figure's name in the word search. Words can be found down, across, and diagonally.

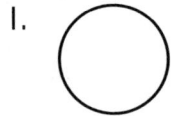

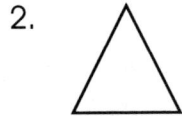

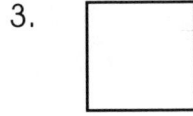

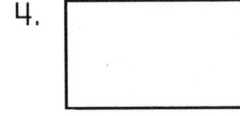

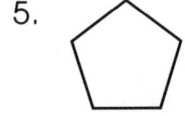

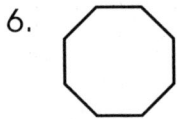

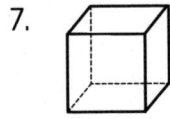

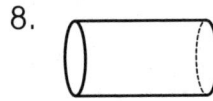

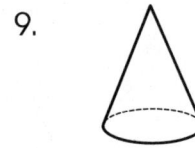

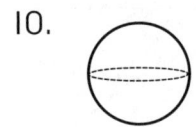

1. (circle)   2. (triangle)   3. (square)   4. (rectangle)   5. (pentagon)

_____   _____   _____   _____   _____

6. (octagon)   7. (cube)   8. (cylinder)   9. (cone)   10. (sphere)

_____   _____   _____   _____   _____

```
I  C  M  K  M  B  Z  S  E  C  P  P  O  A  G  F  R
O  E  A  E  U  U  X  Q  T  H  R  X  L  G  C  P  D
L  M  E  V  L  G  Q  U  C  T  I  R  S  L  Y  Y  S
Z  X  B  X  E  C  Y  L  I  N  D  E  R  W  X  U  P
P  S  X  T  B  H  B  K  O  G  P  E  R  B  V  K  H
I  S  Z  W  R  F  X  E  R  H  C  P  L  A  D  R  E
R  G  P  S  A  I  H  P  B  J  I  R  K  J  I  E  M
W  L  N  H  U  Y  A  L  N  B  R  G  F  N  L  C  F
I  T  S  U  E  A  N  N  W  E  C  T  Y  R  F  T  N
M  D  H  E  S  R  D  Y  G  Z  L  N  T  B  V  A  H
S  P  C  O  R  D  E  L  G  L  E  T  C  J  S  N  H
H  Y  E  U  K  R  W  C  A  G  E  F  P  E  T  G  R
A  R  A  N  B  X  N  P  A  E  K  R  F  E  E  L  N
D  A  C  K  T  E  N  J  C  R  Z  W  R  X  N  E  C
C  G  O  T  H  A  E  F  O  P  X  B  V  A  N  G  K
C  L  N  W  L  Y  G  S  Q  U  A  R  E  R  E  C  Q
S  H  E  D  W  S  D  O  S  L  T  H  G  E  W  P  N
W  Y  M  J  D  I  V  C  N  S  L  K  G  M  P  X  Z
E  U  O  C  T  A  G  O  N  W  D  G  J  B  C  P  O
```

Unwrapped

Triplets Gavin, Gabe, and Ivy are celebrating their birthday. Unfortunately, the gift tags fell off of all of their presents. Identify each three-dimensional figure. Then, use the following clues to write who receives each present.

- Gavin gets all of the gifts shaped like cylinders and cones.
- Gabe gets all of the gifts shaped like cubes and spheres.
- Ivy gets all of the gifts shaped like pyramids, triangular prisms, and rectangular prisms.

1.

_____

_____

2.

_____

_____

3.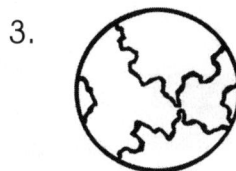

_____

_____

4.

_____

_____

5.

_____

_____

6.

_____

_____

7.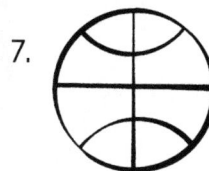

_____

_____

8.

_____

_____

9.

_____

_____

10.

_____

_____

11.

_____

_____

12.

_____

_____

Passing Notes

Kathie received a note from her friend, but half of each letter is missing. To read the note, draw the missing symmetrical half of each letter.

Interior Design

Simi Trey is redecorating her home, and she only wants objects that have symmetry. Help her sort her belongings by drawing a line of symmetry on each object. If the object does not have a line of symmetry, cross it out.

1.

2.

3.

4.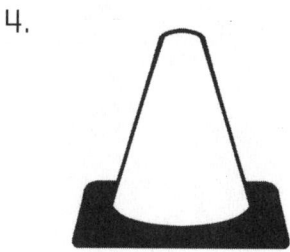

5.

6.

7.

8.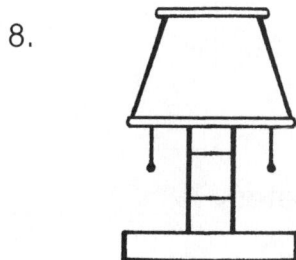

9.

Hanging Out

Find the perimeter of each figure.

1.

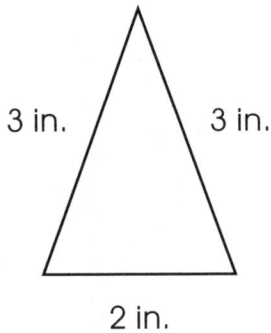

3 in.   3 in.

2 in.

Perimeter = _____

2.

4 yd.

4 yd.   4 yd.

4 yd.

Perimeter = _____

3.

5 mm

6 mm   6 mm

5 mm

Perimeter = _____

4.

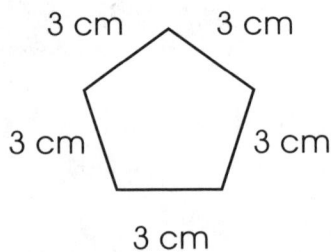

3 cm   3 cm

3 cm   3 cm

3 cm

Perimeter = _____

5.

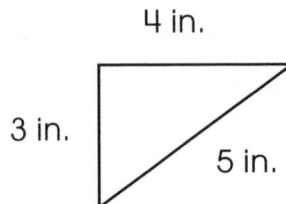

4 in.

3 in.

5 in.

Perimeter = _____

6.

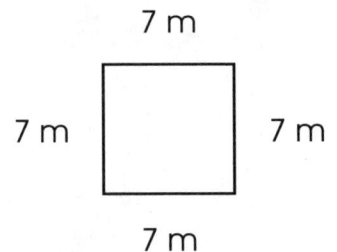

7 m

7 m   7 m

7 m

Perimeter = _____

In the Area

Find the area of each figure.

1.
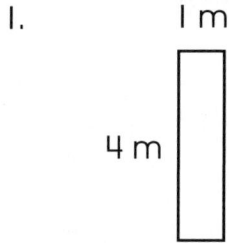

Area = _____

2.
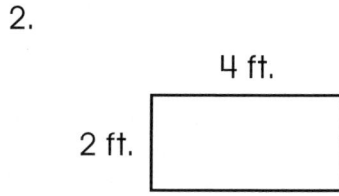

Area = _____

3.
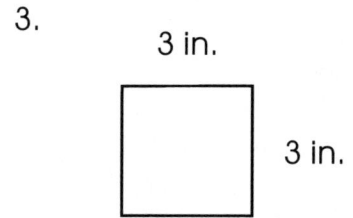

Area = _____

4.
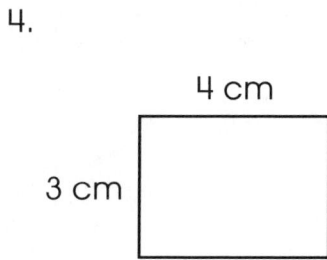

Area = _____

5.
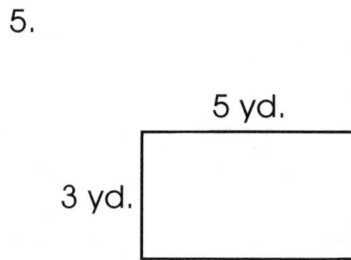

Area = _____

6.
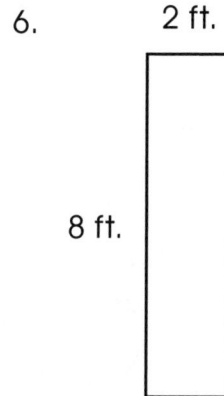

Area = _____

7.
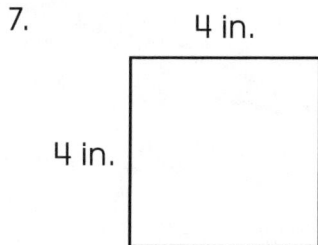

Area = _____

8.
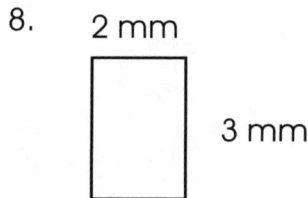

Area = _____

9.
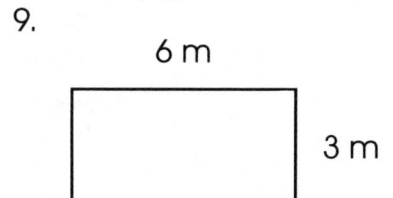

Area = _____

Catch Me If You Can

Find the location of each point on the grid. Match each set of coordinates to the numbers below. To solve the riddle, write the letters in order on the answer lines.

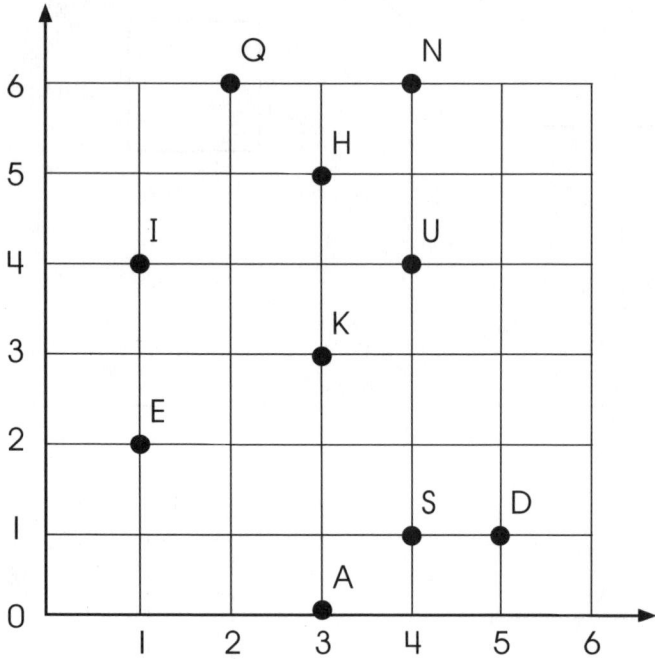

1. Point D (_____ , _____)

2. Point S (_____ , _____)

3. Point A (_____ , _____)

4. Point H (_____ , _____)

5. Point I (_____ , _____)

6. Point Q (_____ , _____)

7. Point U (_____ , _____)

8. Point N (_____ , _____)

9. Point E (_____ , _____)

10. Point K (_____ , _____)

What is a mouse's favorite game?

8..9..10..

Answer: " ___ ___ ___ ___ — ___ — ___ ___ ___ ___ ___ ___ "
　　　　　(3, 5) (1, 4) (5, 1) (1, 2)　(3, 0) (4, 6) (5, 1)　(4, 1) (2, 6) (4,4) (1,2) (3,0) (3,3)

Horsing Around

Write +, −, x, or ÷ to make each equation true.

1. 5 _____ 3 = 15

2. 5 _____ 3 = 8

3. 5 _____ 3 = 2

4. 7 _____ 8 = 15

5. 12 _____ 3 = 4

6. 4 _____ 6 = 24

7. 6 _____ 5 = 11

8. 16 _____ 9 = 7

9. 9 _____ 4 = 36

10. 35 _____ 7 = 5

11. 10 _____ 8 = 18

12. 20 _____ 12 = 8

13. 27 _____ 9 = 3

14. 7 _____ 6 = 13

15. 3 _____ 9 = 27

16. 42 _____ 7 = 6

17. 30 _____ 5 = 6

18. 10 _____ 3 = 7

19. 7 _____ 2 = 14

20. 13 _____ 4 = 9

Opportunity Knocks

Complete each number pattern. To find a Thomas Edison quote, match the answers to the numbers below and write the correct letters on the answer lines. Hint: Some of the letters will be used more than once.

1. 66, ____ , 72, ____ , 78, ____ , 84, 87, ____ , 93
      P   F

2. 14, 21, ____ , ____ , 42, 49, ____ , ____ , ____
            U   D

3. ____ , 20, 24, 28, ____ , ____ , ____ , ____ , 48
   W   A

4. 56, 58, ____ , ____ , ____ , ____ , 68, ____ , 72
           E   Y

5. 30, 36, ____ , ____ , 54, ____ , 66, ____ , ____
           T   G

6. 45, ____ , 55, ____ , 65, ____ , ____ , ____ , 85
          H   L

7. 10, 20, ____ , 40, ____ , ____ , ____ , ____ , ____
         I   S

8. 63, ____ , ____ , 69, ____ , 73, 75, ____ , 79
             O

9. 16, 24, ____ , 40, ____ , ____ , ____ , 72, ____ , 88
                         R

10. ____ , 37, 42, ____ , ____ , 57, ____ , ____ , 72
       N   M

Answer: "___ ___ ___ ___   ___ ___ ___ ___ ___ ___ ___
          72   71   71   63   81   71   80   42   56   47   64

___ ___ ___ ___ ___   ___ ___ ___ ___ ___ ___ ___
71   81   42   64   47   60   32   69   69   64   47   90

___ ___ ___ ___   ___ ___ ___ ___ ___ ___ ___ ___ ___
16   60   64   47   71   69   69   71   80   42   56   47   30   42   66

___ ___ ___ ___ ___   ___ ___ ___ ___
67   64   64   42   90   16   30   42   60

___ ___ ___ ___ ___ ___ ___ ___ .**"**   **– Thomas Edison**
69   75   32   47   47   30   47   72

A New Club

Find the value of n in each problem. To solve the riddle, match the answers to the numbers below and write the correct letters on the answer lines. Hint: All of the letters will not be used, and some of the letters will be used more than once.

1. $52 - n = 39$ **U**
   $n =$ ____

2. $68 - n = 50$ **G**
   $n =$ ____

3. $n \times 6 = 30$ **E**
   $n =$ ____

4. $n + 53 = 121$ **C**
   $n =$ ____

5. $n \div 6 = 6$ **R**
   $n =$ ____

6. $49 \div n = 7$ **A**
   $n =$ ____

7. $2 \div n = 2$ **T**
   $n =$ ____

8. $n + 12 = 12$ **I**
   $n =$ ____

9. $72 - n = 47$ **M**
   $n =$ ____

10. $n \times 1 = 10$ **H**
    $n =$ ____

11. $n - 45 = 22$ **B**
    $n =$ ____

12. $64 \div n = 8$ **S**
    $n =$ ____

13. $n + 95 = 185$ **N**
    $n =$ ____

14. $29 - n = 9$ **O**
    $n =$ ____

15. $10 \times n = 20$ **L**
    $n =$ ____

Why did the golfer need a new club?

Answer: __ __ __ __ __ __ __ __ __ __
67 5 68 7 13 8 5   8 10 5

__ __ __ "__ __ __ __ __ __ __ __ __"
18 20 1   7   10 20 2 5   0 90   20 90 5

Extra Effort

Find the value of _n_ in each problem. Match each answer with the correct letter in the key. To find a Michael Jordan quote, write the letters in order on the answer lines.

0 = E	5 = O	8 = L	10 = N	11 = R	18 = I
24 = G	30 = T	38 = Y	40 = U	54 = A	56 = F

1. $n \div 7 = 8$

    $n = $ _____

2. $n \div 9 = 6$

    $n = $ _____

3. $n + 40 = 58$

    $n = $ _____

4. $40 \div n = 5$

    $n = $ _____

5. $n + 27 = 67$

    $n = $ _____

6. $88 \div n = 8$

    $n = $ _____

7. $n + 14 = 14$

    $n = $ _____

8. $50 \div n = 5$

    $n = $ _____

9. $7 \times n = 35$

    $n = $ _____

10. $n \div 10 = 3$

    $n = $ _____

11. $n - 16 = 14$

    $n = $ _____

12. $12 \times n = 132$

    $n = $ _____

13. $122 - n = 84$

    $n = $ _____

14. $66 + n = 84$

    $n = $ _____

15. $110 \div n = 11$

    $n = $ _____

16. $108 - n = 84$

    $n = $ _____

Answer: "I can accept ____ ____ ____ ____ ____ ____ ____ ;

everyone fails at something. But, I can't accept

____ ____ ____ ____ ____ ____ ____ ____ ____." **– Michael Jordan**

Fishing Trip

Use the order of operations to solve each problem. Match each answer with the correct letter in the key. To solve the riddle, write the letters in order on the answer lines. Hint: The order of operations is multiply or divide, then add or subtract.

0 = O	3 = P	6 = L	8 = A	10 = R	16 = S
18 = U	23 = E	24 = N	27 = H	30 = T	42 = D

1. $3 \times 2 \times 4 =$

2. $15 \div 5 - 3 =$

3. $4 \times 2 + 2 =$

4. $7 \times 3 + 9 =$

5. $9 \times 4 - 9 =$

6. $4 \times 10 \div 5 =$

7. $32 \div 4 \times 3 =$

8. $7 \times 3 \times 2 =$

9. $14 \div 7 \times 8 =$

10. $72 \div 9 - 8 =$

11. $64 \div 8 + 10 =$

12. $18 \div 3 \times 5 =$

13. $3 \times 7 + 6 =$

14. $25 \div 5 - 2 =$

15. $6 \times 2 - 12 =$

16. $42 \div 6 - 1 =$

17. $4 \times 7 - 5 =$

18. $30 \div 3 + 6 =$

What does the earth use to fish?

Answer: ___ ___ ___ ___ ___   ___ ___ ___

"___ ___ ___ ___   ___ ___ ___ ___ ___"

In the Market

Use the order of operations to solve each problem. Match each answer with the correct letter in the key. To solve the riddle, write the letters in order on the answer lines.
Hint: The order of operations is parentheses, multiply or divide, then add or subtract.

6 = A	8 = E	10 = S	14 = T	15 = M
18 = R	21 = F	25 = L	40 = K	

1. $6 + 3 \times 5 =$

2. $(10 - 5) \times 5 =$

3. $28 \div 7 \times 2 =$

4. $9 \times 1 - 3 =$

5. $21 - 3 \times 2 =$

6. $2 + 20 \div 5 =$

7. $4 \times 3 + 6 =$

8. $(5 + 5) \times 4 =$

9. $33 \div 11 + 5 =$

10. $(10 - 3) \times 2 =$

11. $(9 - 4) \times 2 =$

What types of markets do dogs avoid?

SCRATCH

SCRATCH

Answer: "___ ___ ___ ___" ___ ___ ___ ___ ___

Itching to Learn

Find the missing number that makes each equation true. Match each answer with the correct letter in the key. To solve the riddle, write the letters in order on the answer lines.

5 = T	6 = H	8 = C	9 = M	10 = A	11 = I	17 = O	20 = S

1. $19 + 13 + 31 = 7 \times$ _____

2. $103 -$ _____ $= 148 - 62$

3. $39 +$ _____ $= 21 + 23$

4. $48 \div$ _____ $= 100 - 92$

5. $4 \times$ _____ $= 6 \times 6$

6. $81 \div 9 = 19 -$ _____

7. $7 \times 5 = 10 +$ _____ $+ 20$

8. $122 -$ _____ $= 123 - 12$

9. $101 - 37 =$ _____ $\times 8$

10. $24 \div 3 =$ _____ $- 12$

What do insects learn at school?

Answer: " ___ ___ ___ ___ – ___ ___ ___ ___ ___ ___ "

"A-Peeling" Friends

Why are bananas never lonely?

Because they hang around in "bunches."

Use the information below to answer each question.

A fruit basket contains 4 apples, 5 bananas, 12 cherries, 2 peaches, 7 pears, and 5 oranges.

1. What is the probability of pulling out an apple? _____

2. What is the probability of pulling out a banana? _____

3. What is the probability of pulling out a cherry? _____

4. What is the probability of pulling out a peach? _____

5. What is the probability of pulling out a pear? _____

6. What is the probability of pulling out an orange? _____

7. Which fruit are you least likely to pull out? _____

8. You have the same probability of pulling out which two fruits?

_____

9. You have the same probability of pulling out a peach or an orange as you have of pulling out which fruit? _____

10. You have the same probability of pulling out a banana, a peach, or an orange as you have of pulling out which fruit?

_____

Noisemakers

Use the bar graph to answer each question.

Number of Pets Owned

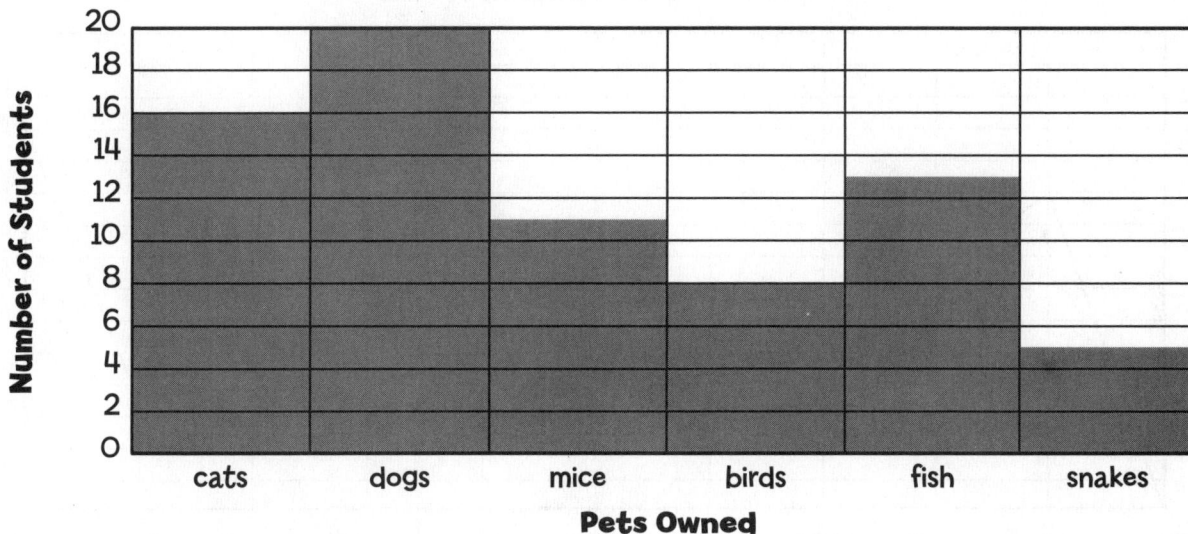

1. Which pet is the most popular? _____

2. Which pet is the least popular? _____

3. How many students own fish? _____

4. How many students own cats? _____

5. Which pets are owned by less than 10 students? _____

Changing Colors

Why did the traffic light turn red?

You would too if you had to "change" in the middle of the street!

The Department of Traffic conducted a study on the amount of traffic on Buckskin Road. Use their line graph to answer each question.

Traffic on Buckskin Road

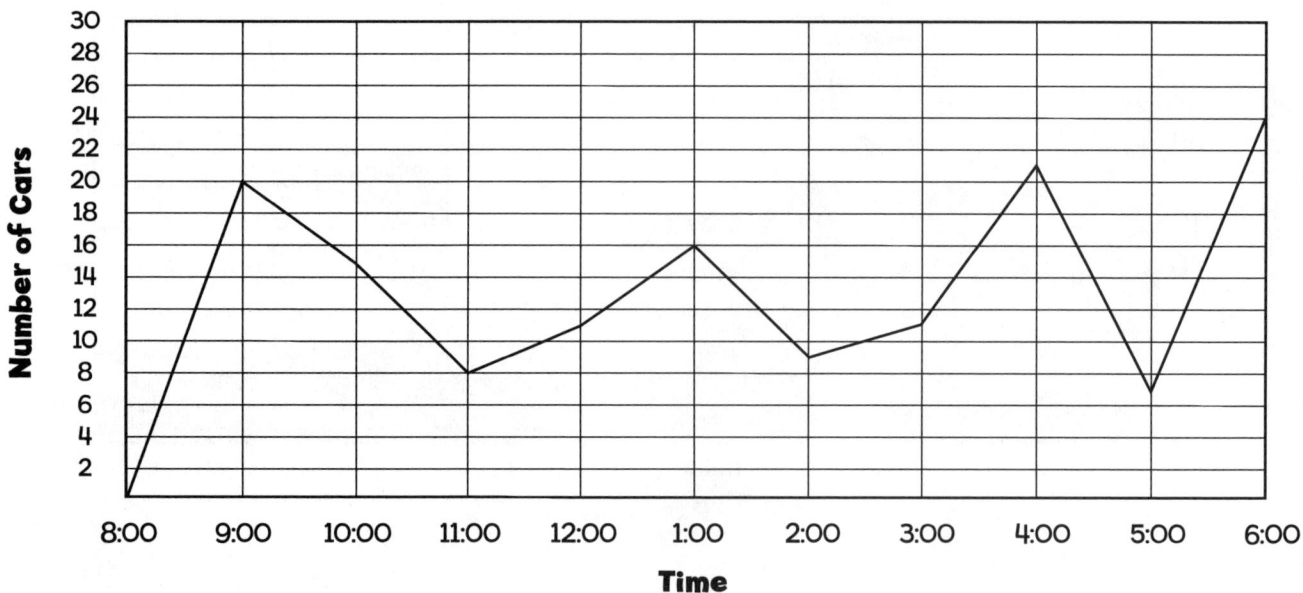

(Line graph: y-axis "Number of Cars" labeled 2 to 30 by 2s; x-axis "Time" labeled 8:00 to 6:00. Data points: 8:00 = 0, 9:00 = 20, 11:00 = 8, 1:00 = 16, 2:00 = 9, 3:00 = 11, 4:00 = 21, 5:00 = 7, 6:00 = 24.)

1. Between which hours was the greatest increase in traffic? _____

2. Between which hours was the greatest decrease in traffic? _____

3. How many fewer cars used Buckskin Road at 11:00 than at 9:00? _____

4. How many more cars used Buckskin Road at 1:00 than at 5:00? _____

5. How many total cars used Buckskin Road from 8:00 to 1:00? _____

Growing Up Too Fast

Why did the elementary student bring a ladder to school?

So that she could go to "high school!"

Use Zany Zoe's class schedule to answer each question.

Zany Zoe's Class Schedule		
7:55 A.M. to 8:24 A.M.	Homeroom	Homeroom
8:30 A.M. to 9:23 A.M.	Period 1	Language Arts
9:29 A.M. to 10:15 A.M.	Period 2	Choir/Art
10:21 A.M. to 11:10 A.M.	Period 3	Science
11:12 A.M. to 12:02 P.M.	Period 4	Health/Gym
12:08 P.M. to 12:55 P.M.	Period 5	Lunch
1:01 P.M. to 1:49 P.M.	Period 6	Math
1:55 P.M. to 2:45 P.M.	Period 7	Social Studies

1. How long is homeroom? _____

2. Which two periods are the same length? _____

3. Which period meets for the longest amount of time? _____

4. Which class, not including homeroom, meets for the shortest amount of time?

   _____

5. Zany Zoe has a doctor's appointment Monday and does not arrive to school until 10:36 A.M. During which class does she arrive? _____

6. On Thursday, Zany Zoe has to leave early. Which class will she miss if she leaves at 1:30 P.M.? Which class will she only miss part of? _____

Page 4

I. >; 2. =; 3. <; 4. <; 5. >; 6. =; 7. >; 8. >; 9. <;
10. <; 11. >; 12. >; 13. <; 14. <; Because they
are smart "kids"

Page 5

I. M; 2. U; 3. L; 4. T; 5. I; 6. P; 7. L; 8. I; 9. E;
10. R; 11. S; "Multi-pliers"

Page 6

I. 590; 2. 460; 3. 1,720; 4. 2,790; 5. 7,870;
6. 880; 7. 340; 8. 3,950; 9. 1,700; 10. 780;
A "sham-poodle"; 11. 900; 12. 800; 13. 700;
14. 3,200; 15. 1,900; 16. 6,100; 17. 4,800;
A "bull-dog"

Page 7

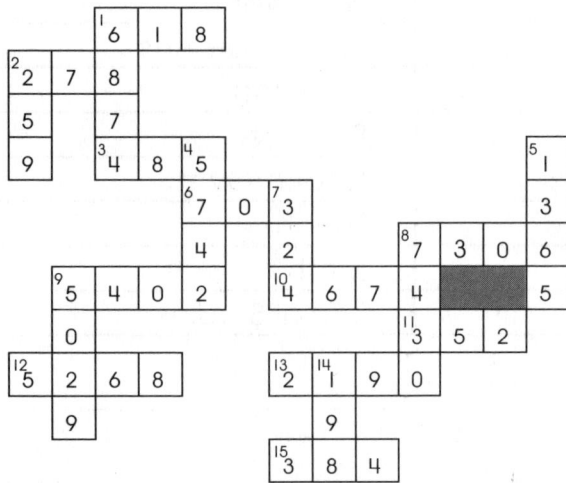

Page 8

I. F; 2. U; 3. R; 4. N; 5. I; 6. T; 7. U; 8. R; 9. E;
"Fur-niture"

Page 9

I. six; 2. fifty; 3. seven; 4. one; 5. three;
6. four; 7. one hundred; 8. two; 9. five;
10. ten; 11. eight; 12. fifteen; 13. twenty;
14. nine

Page 9 (continued)

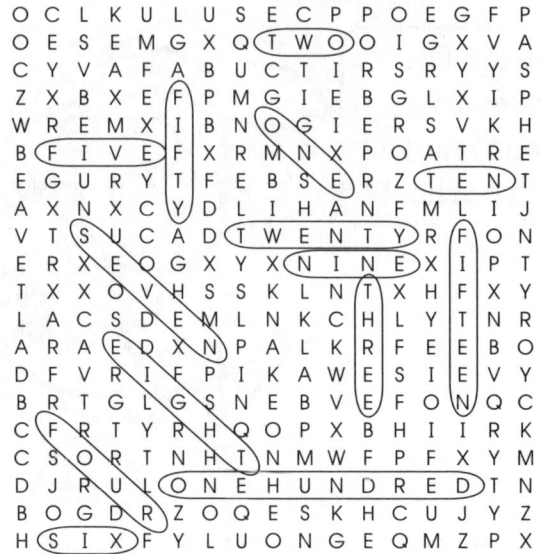

Page 10

I. 172; 2. 131; 3. 84; 4. 147; 5. 45; 6. 68; 7. 81;
8. 150; 9. 613; 10. 589; 11. 572; 12. 827;
13. 482; 14. 925; 15. 721; 16. 558; 17. 744;
18. 941; He was hoping to "loaf" around

Page 11

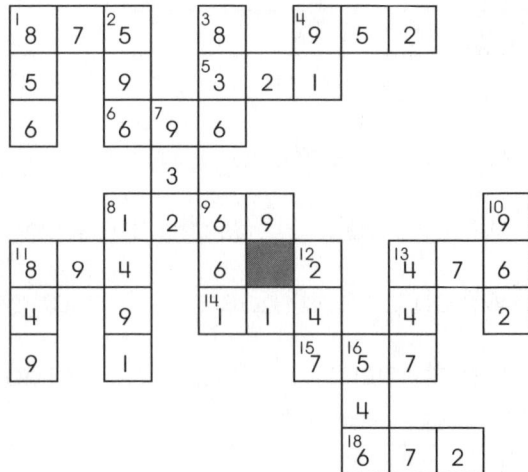

Page 12

I. 7,185; 2. 14,384; 3. 10,099; 4. 7,185;
5. 10,427; 6. 10,099; 7. 11,603; 8. 10,899;
9. 7,185; 10. 15,970; 11. 4,518; 12. 10,427;
A "coat" of paint

Page 13

¹1	1	4	4	6					
3								²5	
5								8	
³1	2	4	6	⁴1				1	
0		0	⁵8	9	5	⁶4	⁷9	9	0	6
8			7			⁸3	6	2	0
7			2			9	■		9
9	⁹7	¹⁰8	1	¹¹9	¹²6	¹³6	0	8	
		2		7		6			
¹⁴7	2	6	9	8		4			
		3		4		7			

Page 14

1. 376; 2. 1,010; 3. 271; 4. 1,612; 5. 899;
6. 1,612; 7. 1,110; 8. 516; 9. 899; 10. 726;
11. 1,249; 12. 516; 13. 1,461; 14. 899; In the
"Hare" Force

Page 15

1. $5.90; 2. $4.29; 3. $7.12; 4. $8.19; 5. $8.37;
6. $3.16; 7. $7.61; 8. $7.93; 9. $6.24; 10. $7.57;
11. $6.88; 12. $8.45; 13. $9.32; 14. $6.92;
15. $8.07; Because they can eat what
"bugs" them

Page 16

1. 7.4; 2. 6.8; 3. 9.9; 4. 5.6; 5. 2.6; 6. 4.6;
7. 7.9; 8. 8.7; 9. 3.9; 10. 5.8; 11. 8.0; 12. 5.9;
13. 7.6; 14. 4.5; 15. 9.4; Because they are
always "spotted"

Page 17

1. 9.63; 2. 14.54; 3. 10.45; 4. 9.36; 5. 7.83;
6. 13.94; 7. 8.93; 8. 6.96; 9. 7.93; 10. 9.56;
11. 10.87; 12. 5.69; 13. 15.69; 14. 8.92;
15. 16.75; Her "furry" godmother

Page 18

1. 463 books; 2. 336 pages; 3. 457 books;
4. 230 pages; 5. $16.97; 6. $13.08

Page 19

1. 7,721 pounds; 2. 19,075 pounds;
3. 3,895 pounds of vegetation;
4. 6,604 gallons of water;
5. 13,592 pounds; 6. 6,513 pounds

Page 20

1. 14; 2. 36; 3. 9; 4. 47; 5. 36; 6. 19; 7. 60;
8. 9; 9. 27; 10. 26; 11. 39; 12. 39; 13. 19;
14. 75; 15. 7; 16. 82; Because they have
"collar" ID

Page 21

¹6	²2	3		³2	⁴4		
⁵6	■	6			8		
7	■	⁶4	⁷2		⁸3	3	
⁹5	¹⁰3	■	¹¹2	8	9	■	¹²7
¹³8	¹⁴5	3		¹⁵1	¹⁶6	0	
	2				3		
¹⁷8	6			¹⁸7	1		
					1		
				¹⁹5	3	4	

Page 22

1. 248; 2. 828; 3. 220; 4. 248; 5. 78; 6. 865;
7. 589; 8. 865; 9. 149; 10. 405; 11. 191; With
"experi-mints"

Page 23

(Crossword grid)

1. 7
2. 202
3. 245
4. 57
6. 65
7. 2
8. 375
9. 5
10. 186
12. 214
13. 1
14. 618
3
16. 19
17. 36
18. 4
3
8
19. 438

Page 24

1. 5,130; 2. 4,773; 3. 7,340; 4. 3,076;
5. 4,003; 6. 2,916; 7. 8,510; 8. 1,252;
9. 9,131; 10. 6,033; 11. 2,602; 12. 5,732;
They "honk" a lot

Page 25

(Crossword grid)

1. 6
2. 3
3. 1278
4. 78
0
6
2
5. 971
4
6. 5764
8. 2
1
10. 340
11. 1
12. 28
0
13. 1
6
14. 6
16. 804
17. 3931
18. 2
19. 47
5
0
20. 4125
3

Page 26

1. $9.03; 2. $1.36; 3. $5.37; 4. $9.03; 5. $1.36;
6. $4.29; 7. $9.03; 8. $9.03; 9. $1.36;
10. $2.40; 11. $5.33; 12. $1.17; 13. $1.24;
14. $9.03; That hit the "spot"

Page 27

1. 2.0; 2. 0.8; 3. 4.7; 4. 4.0; 5. 0.6; 6. 3.7;
7. 1.3; 8. 7.3; 9. 5.3; 10. 7.4; 11. 1.1; 12. 1.6;
13. 3.0; 14. 3.3; 15. 1.5; Because rabbits do
not wear glasses

Page 28

1. 1.81; 2. 2.44; 3. 2.74; 4. 2.83; 5. 0.38;
6. 7.49; 7. 6.21; 8. 3.02; 9. 4.83; 10. 1.61;
11. 2.72; 12. 2.88; 13. 3.11; 14. 5.19; 15. 1.16;
Because her food tasted "funny"

Page 29

1. 64 empty seats; 2. $55.00; 3. $29.99;
4. 2,663 feet; 5. A. 2,084 more hot fudge
sundaes; B. 4,096 more hot fudge
sundaes; 6. A. 1,499 more women;
B. 418 more women

Page 30

1. $15.45; 2. 249 more balloons;
3. $67.19; 4. 1,033 peanuts; 5. A. $14.38;
B. $18.30; 6. A. 207 apples; B. 131 peaches

Page 31

1. 20; 2. 24; 3. 0; 4. 42; 5. 30; 6. 14; 7. 18;
8. 36; 9. 27; 10. 6; 11. 16; 12. 40; 13. 4;
14. 21; 15. 12; He could feel it in his
"bones"

Page 32

1. 70; 2. 77; 3. 144; 4. 24; 5. 40; 6. 24; 7. 36;
8. 60; 9. 60; 10. 32; 11. 24; 12. 72; 13. 56;
14. 36; 15. 40; With "shell" phones

Page 33

1. 28; 2. 129; 3. 66; 4. 450; 5. 35; 6. 300;
7. 124; 8. 45; 9. 84; 10. 249; 11. 105; 12. 99;
13. 75; 14. 102; 15. 128; 16. 208; 17. 305;
18. 216; Where "in earth" have you been?

Page 34

1. 108; 2. 42; 3. 90; 4. 140; 5. 58; 6. 96;
7. 175; 8. 81; 9. 95; 10. 92; 11. 84; 12. 132;
13. 72; 14. 70; 15. 52; Because it is too far
to walk

Page 35

1. 94; 2. 329; 3. 177; 4. 210; 5. 96; 6. 216;
7. 85; 8. 104; 9. 592; 10. 333; 11. 258;
12. 189; 13. 336; 14. 224; 15. 222; 16. 376;
17. 261; 18. 292; Because fish have their
own "scales"

Page 36

1. 32 Low-Fat Fudge Bites;
2. 35 Gingersnap Delights;
3. 15 Marshmallow Puffs; 4. 42 Mighty
Mints; 5. A. 40; B. 42; 6. A. 45; B. 54; C. 63;
D. 72

Page 37

Correct problems: 1, 3, 4, 6, 9, 11, 12, 15, 17,
19, 22, 24; Incorrect problems: 2, 5, 7, 8, 10,
13, 14, 16, 18, 20, 21, 23; When it is "a-jar"

Page 38

1. 3; 2. 7; 3. 5; 4. 3; 5. 1; 6. 8; 7. 9; 8. 6;
9. 11; 10. 12; 11. 4; 12. 7; 13. 4; 14. 2; 15. 1;
16. 10; At parking "meteors"

Page 39

1. 5 packets; 2. 4 packets; 3. A. 4 packets;
B. 5 packets; C. 5 packets; 4. A. 6 packets;
B. 8 packets; C. 9 packets

Page 40

1. $4 \times 6 = 24$, $6 \times 4 = 24$, $24 \div 4 = 6$,
$24 \div 6 = 4$;
2. $6 \times 7 = 42$, $7 \times 6 = 42$, $42 \div 6 = 7$,
$42 \div 7 = 6$;
3. $4 \times 8 = 32$, $8 \times 4 = 32$, $32 \div 4 = 8$,
$32 \div 8 = 4$;
4. $5 \times 9 = 45$, $9 \times 5 = 45$, $45 \div 5 = 9$,
$45 \div 9 = 5$;
5. $7 \times 9 = 63$, $9 \times 7 = 63$, $63 \div 7 = 9$,
$63 \div 9 = 7$;
6. $5 \times 7 = 35$, $7 \times 5 = 35$, $35 \div 5 = 7$,
$35 \div 7 = 5$;
7. $7 \times 8 = 56$, $8 \times 7 = 56$, $56 \div 7 = 8$,
$56 \div 8 = 7$;
8. $6 \times 8 = 48$, $8 \times 6 = 48$, $48 \div 6 = 8$,
$48 \div 8 = 6$;
9. $8 \times 9 = 72$, $9 \times 8 = 72$, $72 \div 8 = 9$,
$72 \div 9 = 8$;
10. $5 \times 8 = 40$, $8 \times 5 = 40$, $40 \div 5 = 8$,
$40 \div 8 = 5$

Page 41

1. $\frac{1}{10}$; 2. $\frac{2}{5}$; 3. $\frac{1}{3}$; 4. $\frac{3}{4}$; 5. $\frac{1}{6}$; 6. $\frac{4}{5}$; 7. $\frac{1}{4}$;
8. $\frac{1}{2}$; 9. $\frac{3}{5}$; 10. $\frac{5}{6}$; A telephone

Page 42

1. >; 2. <; 3. =; 4. <; 5. >; 6. =; 7. <; 8. >;
Vitamin "bee"

Page 43

1. ▪▪▪□□; 2. ●●●○○;

3. ▪□□□; 4. ●●●●●○;

5. ▪▪▪▪□;

6. ●○○○○○; 7. ●●○;

8. ▪□□□□;

9. ●○○○○○○; A yardstick

Page 44

1. May 5; 2. May 17; 3. May 25; 4. May 31;
5. May 2; 6. May 11; 7. May 24; 8. May 14

Page 45

1. 1:50; 2. 4:45; 3. 9:15; 4. 8:10; 5. 2:20

Page 46

1. 35 minutes; 2. 2 hours, 55 minutes;
3. 1 hour, 10 minutes; 4. 1 hour, 40 minutes;
5. 3 hours, 30 minutes; 6. 5 hours,
15 minutes; 7. 45 minutes; 8. 3 hours,
40 minutes; 9. 6 hours; 10. 3 hours,
5 minutes; 11. 4 hours, 10 minutes;
12. 2 hours, 15 minutes; I need my "space"

Page 47

1. D; 2. O; 3. L; 4. L; 5. A; 6. R; 7. S; 8. S; 9. C;
10. E; 11. N; 12. T; 13. S; Dollars and "scents"

Page 48

1. 4 in.; 2. $2\frac{3}{4}$ in.; 3. $10\frac{1}{4}$ in.; 4. $7\frac{1}{2}$ in.;
5. $8\frac{3}{4}$ in.; 6. $3\frac{1}{4}$ in.

Page 49

Answers will vary.

Page 50

1. >; 2. <; 3. >; 4. >; 5. <; 6. >; 7. <; 8. >; 9. <;
10. >; 11. <; 12. <; 13. >; 14. >; 15. <; 16. <;
17. <; Because they have "buck" teeth

Page 51

1. 32°F, 0°C; 2. 77°F, 25°C; 3. 41°F, 5°C;
4. 86°F, 30°C; 5. 68°F, 20°C; 6. 23°F, –5°C

Page 52

1. point, point S; 2. line segment, line
segment AB or $\overline{AB}$; 3. point, point M;
4. ray, ray LM or $\overrightarrow{LM}$; 5. line, line WX or $\overleftrightarrow{WX}$;
6. line segment, line segment QR or $\overline{QR}$;
7. line, line JK or $\overleftrightarrow{JK}$; 8. point, point F;
9. ray, ray CD or $\overrightarrow{CD}$; 10. line segment,
line segment HI or $\overline{HI}$; 11. ray, ray UV or $\overrightarrow{UV}$;
12. point, point Y

Page 53

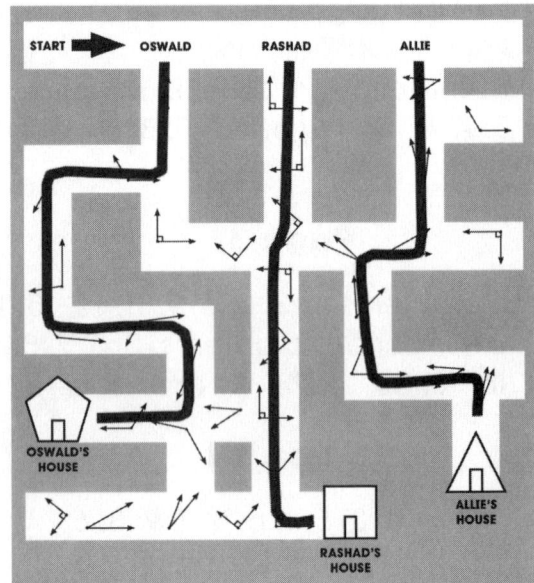

Page 54

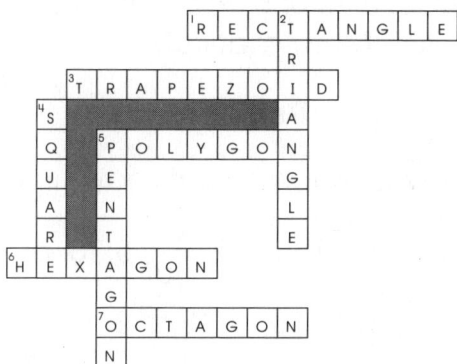

Page 55

Row 1: acute, right, obtuse, obtuse, right, acute, acute; Row 2: obtuse, right, acute, right, obtuse, acute; Row 3: acute, obtuse, right, acute, obtuse, obtuse, acute; Riddle 1: "slippers"; Riddle 2: "cellar-y"; Riddle 3: "pears"

Page 56

1. circle; 2. triangle; 3. square; 4. rectangle; 5. pentagon; 6. octagon; 7. cube; 8. cylinder; 9. cone; 10. sphere

Page 57

1. sphere, Gabe; 2. cylinder, Gavin; 3. sphere, Gabe; 4. rectangular prism, Ivy; 5. triangular prism, Ivy; 6. cylinder, Gavin; 7. sphere, Gabe; 8. cone, Gavin; 9. cube, Gabe; 10. pyramid, Ivy; 11. cylinder, Gavin; 12. cone, Gavin

Page 58

When completed, the page reads *KATHIE, MEET ME AT THE CAVE. DUKE*

Page 59

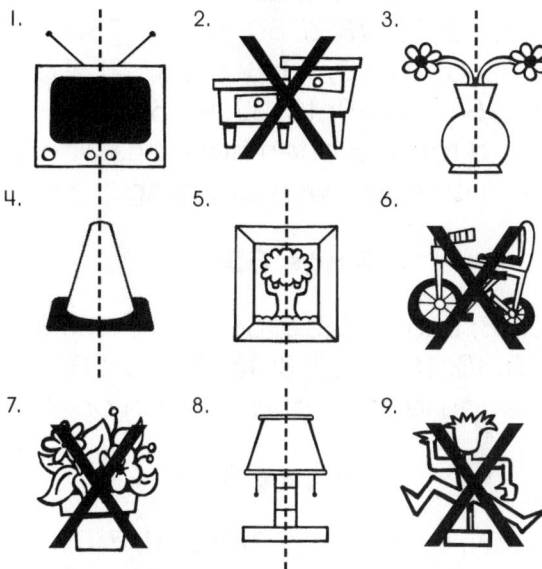

Page 60

1. 8 in.; 2. 16 yd.; 3. 22 mm; 4. 15 cm; 5. 12 in.; 6. 28 m

Page 61

1. 4 m²; 2. 8 ft.²; 3. 9 in.²; 4. 12 cm²; 5. 15 yd.²; 6. 16 ft.²; 7. 16 in.²; 8. 6 mm²; 9. 18 m²

Page 62

1. (5, 1); 2. (4, 1); 3. (3, 0); 4. (3, 5); 5. (1, 4);
6. (2, 6); 7. (4, 4); 8. (4, 6); 9. (1, 2); 10. (3, 3);
"Hide-and-squeak"

Page 63

1. ×; 2. +; 3. −; 4. +; 5. ÷; 6. ×; 7. +; 8. −; 9. ×;
10. ÷; 11. +; 12. −; 13. ÷; 14. +; 15. ×; 16. ÷;
17. ÷; 18. −; 19. ×; 20. −

Page 64

1. 69, 75, 81, 90; 2. 28, 35, 56, 63, 70;
3. 16, 32, 36, 40, 44; 4. 60, 62, 64, 66, 70;
5. 42, 48, 60, 72, 78; 6. 50, 60, 70, 75, 80;
7. 30, 50, 60, 70, 80, 90; 8. 65, 67, 71, 77;
9. 32, 48, 56, 64, 80; 10. 32, 47, 52, 62,
67; "Good fortune often happens when
opportunity meets with planning."

Page 65

1. 13; 2. 18; 3. 5; 4. 68; 5. 36; 6. 7; 7. 1; 8. 0;
9. 25; 10. 10; 11. 67; 12. 8; 13. 90; 14. 20;
15. 2; Because she got a "hole in one"

Page 66

1. 56; 2. 54; 3. 18; 4. 8; 5. 40; 6. 11; 7. 0;
8. 10; 9. 5; 10. 30; 11. 30; 12. 11; 13. 38;
14. 18; 15. 10; 16. 24; "I can accept failure;
everyone fails at something. But, I can't
accept not trying."

Page 67

1. 24; 2. 0; 3. 10; 4. 30; 5. 27; 6. 8; 7. 24;
8. 42; 9. 16; 10. 0; 11. 18; 12. 30; 13. 27;
14. 3; 15. 0; 16. 6; 17. 23; 18. 16; North
and south "poles"

Page 68

1. 21; 2. 25; 3. 8; 4. 6; 5. 15; 6. 6; 7. 18;
8. 40; 9. 8; 10. 14; 11. 10; "Flea" markets

Page 69

1. 9; 2. 17; 3. 5; 4. 6; 5. 9; 6. 10; 7. 5; 8. 11;
9. 8; 10. 20; "Moth-matics"

Page 70

1.–6. Answers will vary but may include:

1. $\frac{4}{35}$, 4:35, or 4 to 35; 2. $\frac{5}{35}$, 5:35, or
5 to 35; 3. $\frac{12}{35}$, 12:35, or 12 to 35;
4. $\frac{2}{35}$, 2:35, or 2 to 35; 5. $\frac{7}{35}$, 7:35, or
7 to 35; 6. $\frac{5}{35}$, 5:35, or 5 to 35; 7. a peach;

8. a banana and an orange; 9. a pear;

10. a cherry

Page 71

1. dogs; 2. snakes; 3. 13 students;
4. 16 students; 5. birds and snakes

Page 72

1. 8:00–9:00; 2. 4:00–5:00; 3. 12 fewer;
4. 9 more; 5. 70 cars

Page 73

1. 29 minutes; 2. Period 4 and Period 7;
3. Period 1; 4. Choir/Art; 5. Science;
6. Social Studies, Math